MASTER THE ART OF GREEKS, COVERED CALLS AND CASH-SECURED PUTS

Copyright © 2024 by Marco Colombo.

All rights reserved. No part of this book may be used or reproduced in any form whatsoever without written permission except in the case of brief quotations in critical articles or reviews.

Book design by Marco Colombo
Cover design by Marco Colombo (Background Image by kjpargeter on Freepik)

THE OPTION TRADER'S INCOME BLUEPRINT

MASTER THE ART OF GREEKS, COVERED CALLS AND CASH-SECURED PUTS

VOLUME 1

MASTER THE ART OF GREEKS, COVERED CALLS AND CASH-SECURED PUTS

ABOUT THE AUTHOR

I am delighted to present to you my latest work, a comprehensive guide to mastering option income strategies. As an experienced professional with a multifaceted background in finance, academia, and investing, I bring a wealth of knowledge and practical insights to this book. Allow me to share a bit about my journey and the expertise that underpins this endeavor.

Professional Background

My career spans several years in the banking sector, where I have held various influential roles, mainly in credit risk management area. My deep understanding of the financial markets was further enriched during my tenure as a capital markets and financial sector consultant. This role allowed me to work closely with industry leaders, providing strategic advice and innovative solutions to complex financial challenges.

Academic Contributions

In addition to my professional experience, I have had the privilege of serving as a professor of statistics and probability at a prestigious university in Italy. Teaching has always been a passion of mine, and through this role, I have been able to inspire and educate the next generation of financial experts. My academic background ensures that the concepts presented in this book are not only practical but also grounded in robust statistical and probabilistic theories.

Investing Experience

Beyond my professional and academic pursuits, I am an avid investor with a diverse portfolio. My real estate investments have provided me with a solid foundation in asset management and long-term financial planning. As a retail investor and trader, particularly in options, I have developed and honed strategies that consistently generate income, even in volatile market conditions.

Purpose of the Book

This book is the culmination of my experiences and knowledge, distilled into a practical guide for anyone looking to harness the power of option income strategies. Whether you are new to options trading or an experienced trader seeking to refine your approach, this book offers valuable insights and step-by-step guidance to help you succeed.

I invite you to embark on this journey with me as we explore the intricacies of options trading and unlock the potential for steady income. With a blend of theoretical knowledge and practical application, this book aims to equip you with the tools and confidence needed to thrive in the world of options trading.

Thank you for your interest in my work. I am confident that the strategies and insights shared in this book will be a valuable addition to your investment toolkit, helping you achieve your financial goals.

DISCLAIMER AND DISCLOSURE

General Disclaimer

The information contained in this series of books, *The Option Trader's Income Blueprint*, is intended for educational purposes only. It is not intended as financial or investment advice, and the author is not a licensed financial advisor. The content provided is based on the author's personal experiences, extensive research, and knowledge gained from various courses and industry analyses. While every effort has been made to ensure the accuracy of the information presented, the author and publisher make no warranties, either express or implied, about the completeness, accuracy, reliability, suitability, or availability of the information, products, services, or related graphics contained in this book for any purpose. Any reliance you place on such information is therefore strictly at your own risk.

Investment Risks

Options trading involves significant risk and is not suitable for every investor. It is possible to lose all or more of your initial investment. Prior to trading options, you should be aware of the risks involved, including the risk of losing your entire investment. It is important to be fully informed about the specific risks associated with trading options and to understand the terms and conditions of your investments. The strategies discussed in this book are designed to generate income, but like all investment strategies, they carry risk. Historical performance is not indicative of future results.

No Financial Advice

The content of this book should not be construed as financial or investment advice. The author does not provide personalized investment advice and is not a qualified licensed investment advisor. The strategies and opinions expressed in this book are solely those of the author and do not constitute specific recommendations or advice for any individual investor. Readers are encouraged to seek professional advice tailored to their individual needs and circumstances before making any investment decisions.

Research and Sources

This book is a collection of in-depth analyses and insights derived from various courses, research, and the author's personal experiences. The material presented, including stock and option prices, has been carefully researched and compiled to provide accurate and valuable information to the reader. However, the dynamic nature of the financial markets means that the information, particularly the specific stock and option prices discussed, may become outdated or less relevant over time. Readers are encouraged to stay informed about the latest market developments, price movements, and to continue their own research beyond the scope of this book to ensure their strategies remain effective.

Personal Responsibility

The strategies and techniques outlined in this book require careful consideration and are to be used at the reader's own risk. The author and publisher disclaim any liability for any direct, indirect, consequential, or incidental losses or damages arising from the use of the information contained in this book. It is the responsibility of the reader to independently verify the information presented and to make informed decisions based on their own judgment and due diligence.

Acknowledgements

The author acknowledges the contributions of various educational courses, industry research, and personal experiences that have enriched the content of this book. The sharing of these insights aims to provide a comprehensive and practical guide to options trading, drawing from a wide range of resources and expertise.

By reading this book, you agree to the terms of this disclaimer and disclosure. Thank you for your understanding and for joining this journey into the world of options trading.

TABLE OF CONTENTS

Introduction: Unlocking the Power of Option Income Strategies 10
    Purpose 10
    Overview 12
    Your Journey to Financial Success 13

Chapter 1: Understanding Options Basics 14
    1.1 Definition and Types of Options (Calls and Puts) 14
    1.2 How Options Trading Differs from Stock Trading 22
    1.3 Key Terms (Strike Price, Expiration Date, Premiums, etc.) 22
    1.4 Greeks 24
    1.5 Practical Advice for Beginners 39
    1.6 Conclusion 40

Chapter 2: Volatility and Options: Understanding the Relationship and Strategies 41
    2.1 Historical Volatility 41
    2.2 Implied Volatility 43
    2.3 Comparing Historical and Implied Volatility 45
    2.4 Mean-Reverting Nature of Volatility 45
    2.5 Implied Volatility Rank and Percentile 47
    2.6 Volatility Skew 50
    2.7 Volatility Surface 53
    2.6 Conclusion 54

Chapter 3: The Fundamentals of Option Income Strategies 56
    3.1 The Concept of Option Income Strategies 56
    3.2 Overview of Income Strategies 57
    3.3 Benefits and Risks of Using Options for Income 59
    3.4 Statistical Edge 60
    3.5 Conclusion 62

Chapter 4: Strategic Asset Selection for Option Income Strategies 64

4.1 Underlying Assets for Option Income Strategies 64

4.2 Quantitative Techniques for Volatility Assessment 69

4.3 Return Metrics and Risk-Adjusted Performance 72

4.4 Liquidity Analysis 74

4.5 Fundamental Analysis 75

4.6 Conclusion 79

Chapter 5: Covered Calls – The Cornerstone of Option Income 80

5.1 The Purpose of Covered Calls 81

5.2 Step-by-Step Guide to Executing a Covered Call 82

5.3 Managing Covered Calls 89

5.4 Adjusting Covered Calls 90

5.5 Estimating Capital Requirements 94

5.6 Conclusion 95

Chapter 6: Cash-Secured Puts – Earning While You Wait 96

6.1 The Purpose of Cash Secured Puts 97

6.2 Step by step guide to executing a Cash Secured Put 98

6.3 Managing Cash-Secured Puts 105

6.4 Adjusting Cash Secured Puts 107

6.5 Estimating Capital Requirements for Cash-Secured Puts 111

6.6 Conclusion 113

Conclusion: Harnessing the Power of Option Income Strategies 114

Annex 117

The Black-Scholes and Binomial Models for Option Pricing 117

Alpha, Beta and the Capital Asset Pricing Model (CAPM) 124

Downside Deviation 127

Glossary 129

Table of Figures 146

Bibliography 147

MASTER THE ART OF GREEKS, COVERED CALLS AND CASH-SECURED PUTS

INTRODUCTION

UNBLOCKING THE POWER OF OPTION INCOME STRATEGIES

Imagine starting each day with the assurance that your investments are working tirelessly, providing a consistent income stream regardless of market fluctuations. Envision attaining financial freedom, not just through traditional stock dividends, but through a powerful yet often misunderstood tool: options. This scenario is not merely a dream but a reality that many traders have achieved by mastering option income strategies.

Options trading offers a unique opportunity to generate reliable income, providing a way to enhance your financial future beyond the limitations of conventional investments. Many traders have found financial success through options, leveraging these instruments to create consistent income streams. However, mastering options trading is a journey that demands a solid understanding of the fundamentals, disciplined risk management, and the ability to adapt to changing market conditions.

This journey isn't without its challenges, but with the right knowledge and strategies, it is one that can lead to profound financial independence. By dedicating yourself to learning and applying the principles of options trading, you too can unlock the potential for consistent, reliable income.

PURPOSE

The Option Trader's Income Blueprint is a comprehensive series designed to equip you with the knowledge, strategies and quantitative methods needed to master the world of options trading. Whether you are a novice eager to explore the possibilities of generating income through options or an experienced trader looking to refine your skills, this series has been meticulously crafted to serve as your ultimate guide.

Options trading can be both rewarding and complex, with a steep learning curve that often deters beginners and challenges even seasoned traders. Recognizing this, *The Option Trader's Income Blueprint* is divided into multiple volumes, each focusing on specific aspects of options trading. By breaking down the material into manageable, topic-focused books, this series ensures that you build a solid foundation before progressing to more advanced strategies.

Each volume in this series addresses a particular facet of options trading, from the basics of understanding options and market dynamics to advanced strategies that can help you consistently generate income. At the time of writing, here's how the series is structured (additional volumes can be potentially added in the future):

- **[Volume 1] Master the Art of Greeks, Covered Calls and Cash Secured Puts:** This volume introduces the essential concepts of options trading, focusing on understanding the Greeks, and mastering foundational income strategies like covered calls and cash-secured puts. You'll learn how to use these tools to generate consistent income while managing risk effectively.

- **[Volume 2] Unleash the Power of Advanced Income Strategies:** Delve into more sophisticated options strategies designed to enhance your income potential. This book covers advanced techniques such as spreads, straddles, iron condors and many others, offering insights on how to implement these strategies to maximize returns. Systematic strategies like the Wheel and its alternative versions will be clearly described together with real examples.

- **[Volume 3] Strategic Adjustments and Quantitative Risk Management:** This title focuses on refining your trading strategies by making strategic adjustments and applying quantitative risk management principles. Learn how to adapt your positions in response to market changes and protect your portfolio from unforeseen risks.

- **[Volume 4] Tools and Market Strategies for a Thriving Options Business:** Explore the tools and market strategies that are essential for building and sustaining a successful options trading business. From selecting the right trading platforms to understanding market trends, this book equips you with the knowledge needed to thrive in the options market.

The series of books is designed so that each volume can stand on its own with internal consistency. However, for the best experience and a deeper understanding of the overarching narrative, it is recommended to read the books in sequential order. Each volume builds on the last, ensuring that your knowledge deepens as you progress through the series, culminating in a comprehensive mastery of options trading. By the time you complete this series, you will have gained not only a thorough understanding of options trading but also the confidence and practical skills to apply these strategies effectively in real-world scenarios.

The Option Trader's Income Blueprint is more than just a collection of books; it's a strategic pathway to financial independence through options trading. So, get ready to embark on this journey, and let's begin by laying the foundation that will support your future success in the options market.

OVERVIEW

Throughout the chapters of this book, you will embark on a journey from understanding the basics of options to mastering covered calls and cash-secured puts. Here's a brief outline of what you will learn:

- **Understanding Options Basics**: We will lay the foundation by explaining what options are and how they work. You will learn about the different types of options, key terms, and the essential concepts that underpin options trading.

- **Volatility and Options: Understanding the Relationship and Strategies**: This chapter explores the relationship between volatility and options, covering historical and implied volatility, their calculations, and mean reversion. It offers strategies for trading during high implied volatility to optimize returns with practical examples and actionable insights.

- **The Fundamentals of Option Income Strategies**: We will introduce the concept of generating income through options, covering basic strategies such as covered calls and cash-secured puts. You will understand the benefits and risks associated with these strategies and learn how to select the right stocks and options.

- **Strategic Asset Selection for Option Income Strategies:** This chapter describe how to identify optimal underlying assets to maximize returns. It explores risk-adjusted returns and the impact of asset volatility, emphasizing the importance of fundamental analysis in asset evaluation. Liquidity is assessed to ensure efficient execution, while quantitative methods are introduced to support decision-making.

- **Covered Calls – The Cornerstone of Option Income**: This chapter will dive deep into the covered call strategy, providing a step-by-step guide to executing it. You will learn how to select the right stocks, manage your positions for maximum profit, and adjust your trades as needed.

- **Cash-Secured Puts – Earning While You Wait**: Explore the cash-secured put strategy as an alternative to covered calls. This chapter will guide you through the process of executing cash-secured puts, selecting the right stocks, and managing your positions effectively.

Your Journey to Financial Success

As you embark on this journey, remember that the path to financial success through options trading is not without its challenges. It requires dedication, continuous learning, and a disciplined approach. However, the rewards—both financial and personal—are well worth the effort.

The Option Trader's Income Blueprint is your essential guide to unlocking the potential of options for generating steady income.

By the end of this book, you will have a solid understanding of key option income strategies, such as covered calls and cash-secured puts, along with a firm grasp of the Greeks. With practical advice, real-life examples, and step-by-step guides, this volume will equip you with the foundational knowledge needed to start generating consistent income through options trading.

Take the first step towards transforming your financial future. Let's unlock the potential of options trading together and build a blueprint for your success.

CHAPTER 1

UNDERSTANDING OPTION BASICS

The goal of this chapter is to lay a solid foundation for your journey into the world of options buying and selling. Before diving into strategies and methods, it's essential to understand the main concepts that underpin options trading. Your success as an options trader depends on a thorough grasp of the basics.

Options trading can seem complex and intimidating at first, but with the right approach and a solid understanding of key concepts, it can become a powerful addition to your investment toolkit. This chapter aims to demystify options trading, breaking down complex concepts into manageable and actionable steps. By the end of this chapter, you will have a clear understanding of what options are, how they work, and the essential terminology and principles needed to navigate the options market confidently.

1.1 Definition and Types of Options (Calls and Puts)

Options are financial derivatives that derive their value from an underlying asset, such as stocks, indices, or commodities. An option contract gives the holder the right, but not the obligation, to buy or sell the underlying asset at a predetermined price, known as the strike price, within a specified period. There are two primary types of options: call options and put options.

1.1.1 Call Options

A call option gives the holder the right to buy an asset at the strike price before the option expires. Investors purchase call options when they believe the price of the underlying asset will rise above the strike price before the expiration date.

Let's say you are bullish on Company ABC, currently trading at $100 per share. You believe that within the next three months, ABC's stock price will increase significantly due to an anticipated positive earnings report.

- **Strike Price**: $110
- **Expiration Date**: Three months from today
- **Premium**: $5 per share

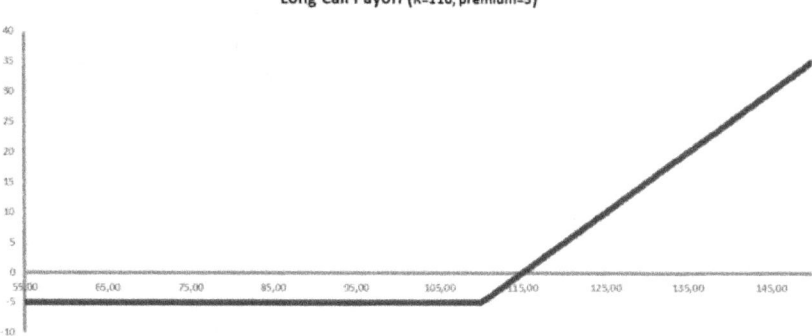

Figure 1 - Long Call Payoff

You purchase a call option for 100 shares (standard contract size) with a strike price of $110, expiring in three months, at a premium of $5 per share. This purchase costs you $500 (100 shares * $5 per share).

Possible Outcomes:

- **Stock Price Rises to $130**: Your call option is now "in the money" because the stock price ($130) is above the strike price ($110). You exercise your option to buy the shares at $110 each and can sell them at the current market price of $130. Your profit is calculated as follows:
    - Profit per share: $130 - $110 - $5 (premium) = $15
    - Total profit: 100 shares * $15 = $1,500

- **Stock Price Rises to $115**: Your call option is still "in the money." You can exercise your option to buy the shares at $110 and sell them at $115.
    - Profit per share: $115 - $110 - $5 (premium) = $0
    - Total profit: 100 shares * $0 = $0 (You break even, but you have not lost money beyond the premium paid)

- **Stock Price Remains at $100 or Falls**: Your call option expires "out of the money" because the stock price ($100) is below the strike price ($110). The option expires worthless, and you lose the premium paid.
    - Total loss: $500

Selling a call option, also known as writing a call option, involves entering into a contract where the seller (writer) of the option agrees to sell a specified quantity of an underlying asset to the buyer of the option at a predetermined price (strike price) within a certain period (expiration date). The chart shows the payoff of a short call with the same features as the ones previously described:

- **Strike Price**: $110

- **Expiration Date**: Three months from today

- **Premium**: $5 per share

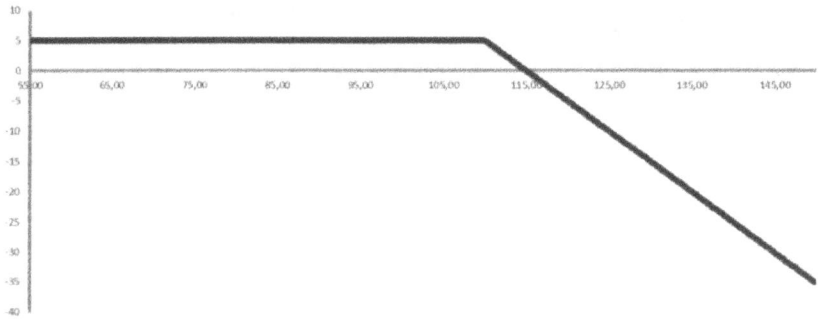

Figure 2 - Short Call Payoff

Here's a detailed breakdown of the process and its implications:

- **Contract Creation**: When you sell a call option, you create an options contract that gives the buyer the right, but not the obligation, to purchase the underlying asset (such as stocks, ETFs, or commodities) from you at the strike price before the option expires.

- **Premium**: In return for writing the call option, you receive a premium from the buyer. This premium is the price of the option, and it is the compensation you receive for taking on the obligation to sell the underlying asset if the buyer exercises the option.

- **Obligation**: As the seller of the call option, you are obligated to sell the underlying asset at the strike price if the buyer chooses to exercise the option. This obligation lasts until the option expires or the buyer decides to exercise it.

- **Strike Price and Expiration Date**:
    - **Strike Price**: The price at which the underlying asset can be bought by the option holder.
    - **Expiration Date**: The date by which the option must be exercised or it expires worthless.

- **Scenarios for Selling a Call Option**:
    - **Covered Call:** If you already own the underlying asset, selling a call option against it is known as a covered call. This strategy will be described in the next chapters and generates additional income (the premium) from your holdings. If the option is exercised, you will sell your underlying asset at the strike price.
    - **Naked Call:** If you do not own the underlying asset, selling a call option is known as a naked call. This strategy is riskier because if the option is exercised, you will need to buy the underlying asset at the current market price to sell it at the lower strike price, potentially resulting in significant losses.

- **Profit and Loss**:

- **Profit**: As the seller, your maximum profit is the premium received for writing the call option. This profit is realized if the option expires worthless (i.e., the market price of the underlying asset stays below the strike price until expiration).
- **Loss**: The potential loss can be substantial, especially in a naked call scenario. If the underlying asset's market price rises significantly above the strike price, you may incur large losses, as you will be forced to sell the asset at the strike price, which is lower than the market price.

1.1.2 Put Options

A put option gives the holder the right to sell an asset at the strike price before the option expires. Investors buy put options when they believe the price of the underlying asset will fall below the strike price before the expiration date.

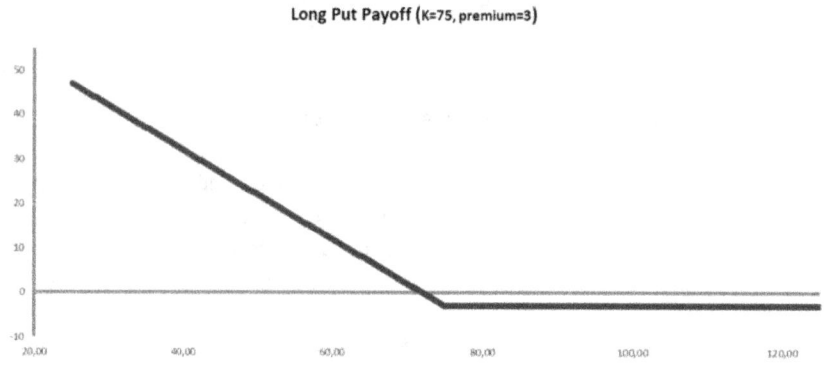

Figure 3 - Long Put Payoff

Suppose you are bearish on Company XYZ, currently trading at $80 per share. You anticipate that XYZ's stock price will decline due to unfavorable market conditions.

- **Strike Price**: $75
- **Expiration Date**: Two months from today

- **Premium**: $3 per share

You purchase a put option for 100 shares with a strike price of $75, expiring in two months, at a premium of $3 per share. This purchase costs you $300 (100 shares * $3 per share).

Possible Outcomes:

- **Stock Price Falls to $60**: Your put option is "in the money" because the stock price ($60) is below the strike price ($75). You exercise your option to sell the shares at $75 each while they are currently worth $60.
    - Profit per share: $75 - $60 - $3 (premium) = $12
    - Total profit: 100 shares * $12 = $1,200

- **Stock Price Falls to $70**: Your put option is still "in the money." You can exercise your option to sell the shares at $75 while they are worth $70.
    - Profit per share: $75 - $70 - $3 (premium) = $2
    - Total profit: 100 shares * $2 = $200

- **Stock Price Remains at $80 or Rises**: Your put option expires "out of the money" because the stock price ($80) is above the strike price ($75). The option expires worthless, and you lose the premium paid.
    - Total loss: $300

Selling a put option, also known as writing a put option, involves entering into a contract where the seller (writer) of the option agrees to buy a specified quantity of an underlying asset from the buyer of the option at a predetermined price (strike price) within a certain period (expiration date). The chart shows the payoff of a short call with the same features as the ones previously described:

- **Strike Price**: $75

- **Expiration Date**: Two months from today

- **Premium**: $3 per share

MASTER THE ART OF GREEKS, COVERED CALLS AND CASH-SECURED PUTS

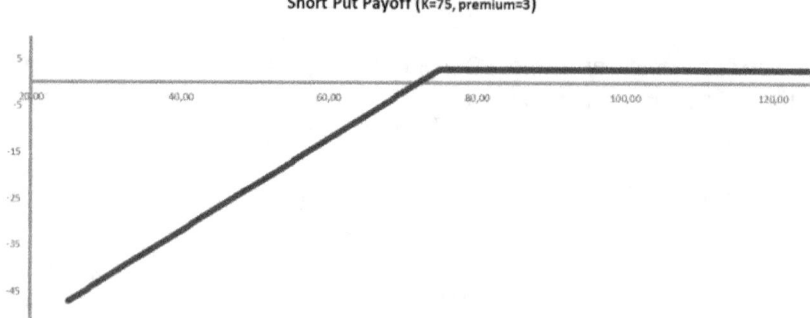

Figure 4 - Short Put Payoff

Here's a detailed breakdown of the process and its implications:

- **Contract Creation**: When you sell a put option, you create an options contract that gives the buyer the right, but not the obligation, to sell the underlying asset (such as stocks, ETFs, or commodities) to you at the strike price before the option expires.

- **Premium**: In return for writing the put option, you receive a premium from the buyer. This premium is the price of the option, and it is the compensation you receive for taking on the obligation to buy the underlying asset if the buyer exercises the option.

- **Obligation**: As the seller of the put option, you are obligated to buy the underlying asset at the strike price if the buyer chooses to exercise the option. This obligation lasts until the option expires or the buyer decides to exercise it.

- **Strike Price and Expiration Date**:
    - **Strike Price**: The price at which the underlying asset can be sold by the option holder.
    - **Expiration Date**: The date by which the option must be exercised or it expires worthless.

- **Scenarios for Selling a Call Option**:
    - **Cash-Secured Put:** If you have sufficient cash set aside to buy the underlying asset at the strike price if the option is exercised, this is known as selling a cash-secured put. This

strategy will be described in the next chapter and allows you to earn income (the premium) and potentially buy the underlying asset at a discount if its price falls below the strike price.
- **Naked Put:** If you do not have sufficient cash set aside, selling a put option is known as a naked put. This strategy is riskier because if the option is exercised and the underlying asset's price falls significantly, you will need to come up with the cash to buy the asset at the higher strike price, leading to potential losses.

- **Profit and Loss:**
  - **Profit:** As the seller, your maximum profit is the premium received for writing the put option. This profit is realized if the option expires worthless (i.e., the market price of the underlying asset stays above the strike price until expiration).
  - **Loss:** The potential loss can be substantial if the underlying asset's market price falls significantly below the strike price. You will be forced to buy the asset at the strike price, which is higher than the market price, potentially leading to significant losses.

1.1.3 Comparing Call and Put Options

While call and put options function differently, they both offer strategic advantages depending on market expectations:

- **Call Options:** Use when you expect the price of the underlying asset to increase. It allows you to leverage your position and potentially generate higher returns than directly buying the asset.

- **Put Options:** Use when you expect the price of the underlying asset to decrease. It provides a way to profit from declining prices or hedge against potential losses in your portfolio.

When trading options, it is essential to consider the following factors:

- **Volatility**: Options are more valuable in volatile markets because there is a higher probability that the underlying asset's price will move significantly.

- **Time Decay**: The value of options decreases as the expiration date approaches, a phenomenon known as time decay. The longer the time until expiration, the higher the premium, as there is more time for the underlying asset's price to move favorably.

- **Liquidity**: Highly liquid options markets ensure that you can easily enter and exit positions without significant price impact.

1.2 How Options Trading Differs from Stock Trading

While stock trading involves buying and selling shares of a company, options trading involves contracts based on the underlying stock. This distinction brings about several key differences:

- **Leverage**: Options allow traders to control a large position with a relatively small amount of money. This leverage can amplify both gains and losses.

- **Flexibility**: Options can be used to implement a variety of strategies, from hedging to speculation, providing greater flexibility than stock trading.

- **Risk Management**: Options can be used to manage risk more effectively, such as through protective puts or covered calls.

1.3 Key Terms (Strike Price, Expiration Date, Premiums, etc.)

Understanding the language of options is essential for effective trading. Here are some key terms already described in the previous chapters that you need to know:

- **Strike Price**: The price at which the holder can buy (call) or sell (put) the underlying asset.
    - **At the Money**: An option is considered At-The-Money if the strike price is approximately equal to the current market price of the underlying asset. The premium mostly

consists of time value since the option has little to no intrinsic value.
- **Out of the Money**: An option is Out-of-The-Money if it has no intrinsic value. This means the strike price is not favorable compared to the current market price of the underlying asset (current price < strike for calls and current price > strike for puts). The premium is mainly time value with no intrinsic value, making them cheaper and riskier.
- **In the Money**: An option is In-The-Money if it has intrinsic value. This means the strike price is favorable compared to the current market price of the underlying asset (current price > strike for calls and current price < strike for puts). The premium consists of intrinsic value plus time value, making them more expensive.

- **Expiration Date**: The date by which the option must be exercised or it will expire worthless.

- **Premium**: The price paid for the option contract, reflecting the cost of the option's rights.

- **Intrinsic Value**: The difference between the underlying asset's current price and the strike price.

- **Time Value**: The portion of the option's premium attributable to the amount of time remaining until expiration.

- **Settlement**:
  - **Physical Settlement:** Stock and ETF options typically settle through a process known as "physical settlement." In this method, the actual shares of the underlying stock or ETF are transferred between the buyer and seller of the option when the option is exercised.
  - **Cash Settlement:** Index options do not involve the delivery of physical assets because an index itself cannot be bought or sold like a stock. Instead, these options are settled in cash based on the difference between the option's strike price and the settlement value of the index.

- **European / American Option**:

- **European**: European options are financial derivatives that can only be exercised on their expiration date. This means that the holder of a European option cannot exercise the option at any point before the option's maturity. Often used for index options and some exotic options.
- **American**: American options are financial derivatives that can be exercised at any time before or on the expiration date. This flexibility allows the holder to capitalize on favorable movements in the underlying asset's price at any point during the life of the option. Predominantly used for individual stock and ETF options (most used ones).

1.4 GREEKS

The Greeks are essential tools for measuring the risks and potential rewards of an options position. Each Greek provides insight into how different factors affect an option's price:

- **Delta**: Measures the sensitivity of the option's price to changes in the underlying asset's price.

- **Gamma**: Measures the rate of change of Delta with respect to changes in the underlying asset's price.

- **Theta**: Measures the sensitivity of the option's price to the passage of time, often referred to as time decay.

- **Vega**: Measures the sensitivity of the option's price to changes in the volatility of the underlying asset.

- **Rho**: Measures the sensitivity of the option's price to changes in interest rates.

The next paragraphs will provide details about each Greek reported above, showing also the mathematical background and formulas for sake of completeness. The trader should be aware that all the new trading platforms provide the mentioned Greek for each option contract available, thus avoiding the effort needed to compute them.

1.4.1 Delta

Delta measures the sensitivity of an option's price to changes in the price of the underlying asset. Specifically, it indicates how much the price of an option is expected to change for a $1 change in the price of the underlying asset. Delta values range from -1 (high sensitivity) to 0 (low sensitivity) for put options and 0 (low sensitivity) to 1 (high sensitivity) for call options.

Delta is approximately 0.5 for ATM options, while it increases (decreases) for ITM (OTM) options.

Mathematically, delta is the first derivative of the option's price with respect to the price of the underlying asset. It provides an estimate of how much the price of an option will change in response to a $1 change in the price of the underlying asset.

The delta can be expressed as:

$$\Delta = \frac{\partial C}{\partial S}$$

Where:
- C is the price of the call option (or P for the put option).
- S is the current price of the underlying asset.

In the context of the Black-Scholes option pricing model (see Annex), the delta for European call and put options can be explicitly calculated using the cumulative distribution function (CDF) of the standard normal distribution, denoted by $N(d_1)$. The formulas are as follows:

For a call option:

$$\Delta_{call} = N(d_1)$$

For a put option:

$$\Delta_{put} = N(d_1) - 1$$

Where d_1 is given by:

$$d_1 = \frac{\ln(\frac{S}{K}) + (r + \frac{\sigma^2}{2})T}{\sigma\sqrt{T}}$$

Where:

- S is the current price of the underlying asset.
- K is the strike price of the option.
- r is the risk-free interest rate.
- σ is the volatility of the underlying asset.
- T is the time to expiration of the option.
- N(d1) represents the probability that the option will expire in the money, assuming a normal distribution of returns.

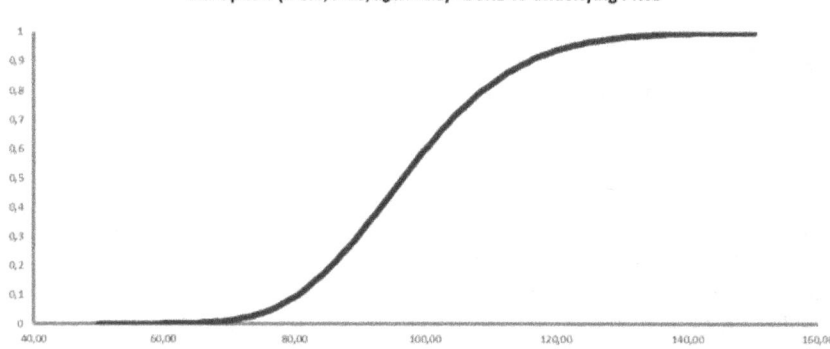

Figure 5 - Call Option - Delta vs Underlying Price

Suppose you own a call option on Company ABC, which is currently trading at $50. The call option has a delta of 0.6.

- **If ABC's stock price rises by $1 to $51**, the price of the call option is expected to increase by approximately $0.60.
- **If ABC's stock price falls by $1 to $49**, the price of the call option is expected to decrease by approximately $0.60.

For put options, delta works in the opposite direction. If you own a put option with a delta of -0.4 and the stock price decreases by $1, the price of the put option is expected to increase by $0.40.

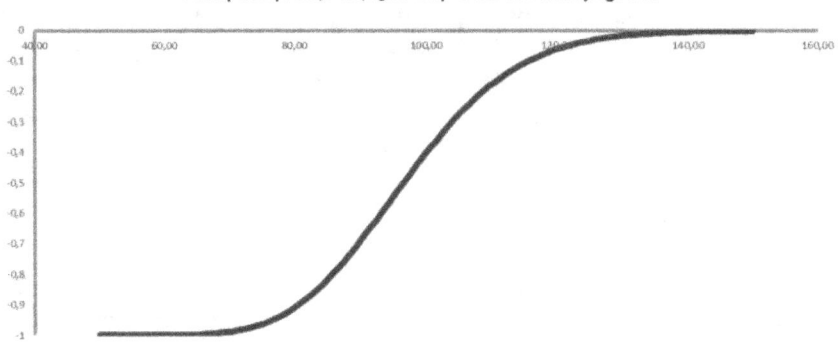

Figure 6 - Put Option - Delta Vs Underlying Price

However, delta serves another critical function beyond its role in pricing — it provides a valuable approximation of an option's probability of expiring in the money. This probabilistic interpretation stems from the fact that delta reflects the option's sensitivity to price changes, which correlates with its moneyness. Here's how delta approximates probability:

For Call Options:

- A call option with a delta of 0.70 implies that there is approximately a 70% chance that the call will end up in the money at expiration.

- This is because as the underlying asset's price rises, the likelihood of the option finishing in the money increases, and a higher delta reflects a higher probability of this outcome.

For Put Options:

- Conversely, a put option with a delta of -0.60 suggests a roughly 60% chance of finishing in the money. The negative delta indicates that as the price of the underlying asset falls, the probability of the put option finishing in the money increases.

Imagine you are considering buying a call option on Stock XYZ, which is currently trading at $50. You are looking at a call option with a strike price of $55, and this option has a delta of 0.30. Here's how to interpret this delta:

- **Probability Estimation:** The delta of 0.30 suggests that there is approximately a 30% chance that Stock XYZ will be above $55 at expiration, making the call option in the money

- **Decision Making:** If you are risk-averse and want higher certainty about the option expiring in the money, you might look for options with a higher delta. Conversely, if you are comfortable with higher risk for potentially higher rewards, you might choose options with lower delta, which reflect lower probabilities of finishing in the money but can offer higher leverage and returns.

Probability of Touching

The probability of touching refers to the likelihood that the underlying asset will reach a particular strike price at any point during the life of the option. This probability is different from the probability of being in-the-money at expiration:

- **Call Options:** The probability of the underlying asset touching the strike price at least once during the life of the option is approximately twice the Delta.

- **Put Options:** Similar logic applies, with the probability of touching for put options being approximately twice the absolute value of the Delta.

Relationship Between Delta and Probability of Touching

The Delta of an option provides insight not only into the likelihood of the option being in-the-money at expiration but also into the dynamics of the underlying asset's price movement during the option's life:

- **Delta as ITM Probability:** If a call option has a Delta of 0.30, there is approximately a 30% chance that it will expire in-the-money.

- **Probability of Touching:** The same option has approximately a 60% chance (2 * Delta) of the underlying asset touching the strike price at least once before expiration.

Understanding the relationship between Delta, the probability of being in-the-money at expiration, and the probability of touching can significantly enhance a trader's strategy and decision-making process.

Example Scenario

Consider a trader who is evaluating a call option on a stock currently trading at $100. The call option has a strike price of $110 and a Delta of 0.25.

- **ITM Probability:** The trader knows there is a 25% chance that the option will be in-the-money at expiration.

- **Touching Probability**: The trader also understands there is roughly a 50% chance that the stock will touch the $110 strike price at some point during the option's life.

Actions based on these insights:

- **Managing Expectations**: By knowing the ITM probability, the trader can set realistic expectations for the option's performance and potential payoff.

- **Risk Management**: Understanding the touching probability helps the trader manage risk. For example, if the trader sells the $110 call option, knowing there's a 50% chance of touching can prepare them for potential price movements and the need for adjustments.

- **Strategy Adjustments**: Traders can use Delta to tailor their strategies. If they seek higher probabilities of profit, they might choose options with higher Deltas. Conversely, for more aggressive strategies with potentially higher rewards, they might opt for options with lower Deltas but higher potential payouts.

- **Volatility Considerations**: Delta changes with volatility. High implied volatility can increase Delta for out-of-the-money options, affecting both ITM and touching probabilities. Traders can adjust their strategies based on these dynamic conditions.

1.4.2 Gamma

Gamma measures the rate of change of Delta with respect to the price of the underlying asset. It helps traders understand how much the Delta is expected to change when the price of the underlying asset moves.

Gamma is always positive for both call and put options. This is because delta is an increasing function for calls and a decreasing function (in absolute terms) for puts as the underlying price increases. Gamma is highest for at-the-money (ATM) options and decreases as the option becomes more in-the-money (ITM) or out-of-the-money (OTM).

Gamma represents the "acceleration" of the option's price in relation to the underlying asset's price. A higher gamma indicates that delta is more sensitive to movements in the underlying asset's price.

ATM options have the highest gamma because they are most sensitive to changes in the underlying asset's price—small changes can significantly alter the probability of the option ending up ITM. Conversely, ITM and OTM options have lower gamma because their deltas are less sensitive to small movements in the underlying asset.

Gamma is mathematically defined as the second derivative of the option's price with respect to the price of the underlying asset, or equivalently, the first derivative of delta with respect to the price of the underlying asset:

$$\Gamma = \frac{\partial \Delta}{\partial S} = \frac{\partial^2 C}{\partial S}$$

Where:
- C is the price of the call option (or P for the put option.
- S is the current price of the underlying asset.
- Δ is the first derivative of the option price with respect to the underlying asset price.

Gamma is the same for both call and put options, as both share the same curvature in their price behavior relative to changes in the underlying asset's price.

In the Black-Scholes option pricing model (see Annex), gamma for both European call and put options is given by:

$$\Gamma = \frac{N'(d_1)}{S\sigma\sqrt{T}}$$

Where:
- $N'(d_1)$ is the probability density function (PDF) of the standard normal distribution, often expressed as:

$$N'(d_1) = \frac{1}{\sqrt{2\pi}} e^{-\frac{d_1^2}{2}}$$

- S is the current price of the underlying asset.
- σ is the volatility of the underlying asset.
- T is the time to expiration of the option.
- d_1 is defined as:

$$d_1 = \frac{\ln(\frac{S}{K}) + (r + \frac{\sigma^2}{2})T}{\sigma\sqrt{T}}$$

Where:
- K is the strike price of the option.
- r is the risk-free interest rate.

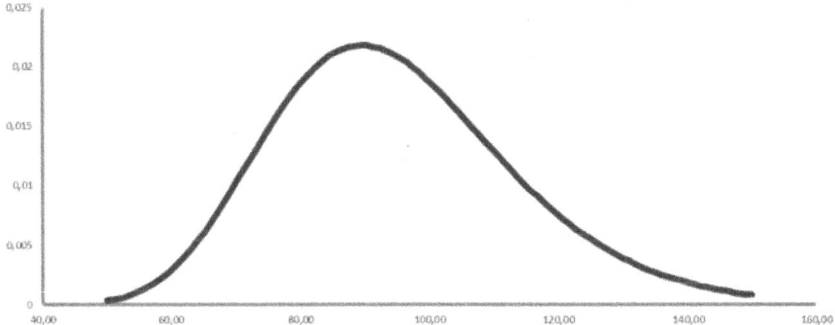

Figure 7 - Call/Put Option - Gamma vs Underlying Price

Suppose a call option on ABC has a gamma of 0.05.

- **If ABC's stock price increases by $1 from $50 to $51**, the Delta of the call option will increase from 0.6 to 0.65 (0.6 + 0.05).
- **If ABC's stock price decreases by $1 from $50 to $49**, the Delta of the call option will decrease from 0.6 to 0.55 (0.6 - 0.05).

1.4.3 Theta

Theta measures the sensitivity of an option's price to the passage of time, also known as time decay. Theta reflects the erosion of an option's extrinsic value as time passes and it indicates how much the price of an option is expected to decrease per day as it approaches expiration.

It is usually expressed as a negative number because the value of options tends to decrease over time.

Theta relationship with DTE and ATM:

- Shorter DTE (Days to Expiration): Options with shorter expiration periods experience faster theta decay. By selecting options with shorter DTE, traders can capture more premium decay in a shorter period.

- Higher Theta Options: Options closer to at-the-money (ATM) generally have higher theta values. Selling ATM options can enhance income from theta decay, though this comes with higher risk if the underlying asset moves significantly.

Theta plays a crucial role in the success of option income strategies.

Mathematically, theta is defined as the partial derivative of the option's price with respect to time:

$$\theta = \frac{\partial C}{\partial t}$$

Where:
- C is the price of the call option (or P for the put option).
- t is the time remaining until the option's expiration.

In the Black-Scholes option pricing model, the theta for a European call option is given by:

$$\theta_{call} = -\frac{S\sigma N'(d_1)}{2\sqrt{T}} - rKe^{-rT}N(d_2)$$

and for a European Put:

$$\theta_{put} = -\frac{S\sigma N'(d_1)}{2\sqrt{T}} + rKe^{-rT}N(-d_2)$$

Where:

- S is the current price of the underlying asset.
- σ is the volatility of the underlying asset.
- T is the time to expiration of the option.
- K is the strike price of the option.
- r is the risk-free interest rate.
- $N(\cdot)$ is the cumulative distribution function (CDF) of the standard normal distribution.
- $N'(d_1)$ is the probability density function (PDF) of the standard normal distribution, and is calculated as:

$$N'(d_1) = \frac{1}{\sqrt{2\pi}} e^{-\frac{d_1^2}{2}}$$

- d_1 and d_2 are given by:

$$d_1 = \frac{\ln(\frac{S}{K}) + (r + \frac{\sigma^2}{2})T}{\sigma\sqrt{T}}$$

$$d_2 = d_1 - \sigma\sqrt{T}$$

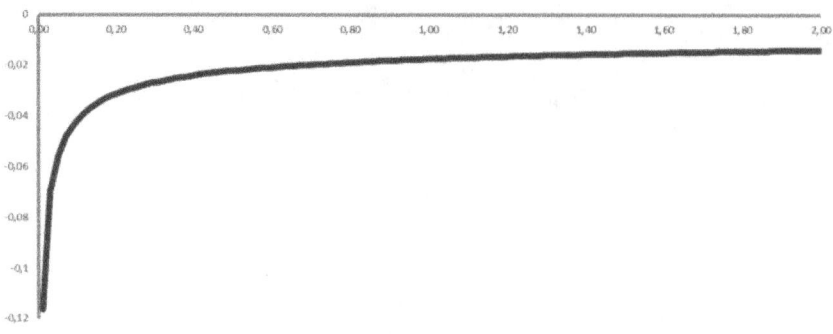

Figure 8 - Call Option - Theta vs DTE

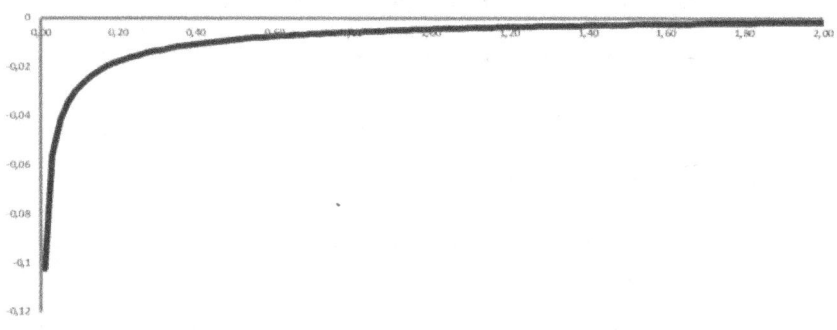

Figure 9 - Put Option - Theta vs DTE

Suppose you own an at-the-money call option on Company XYZ with a Theta of -0.10.

- **Every day that passes**, the price of the call option is expected to decrease by approximately $0.10, assuming all other factors remain constant.

1.4.4 Vega

Vega measures the sensitivity of an option's price to changes in the volatility (see next chapter for further details) of the underlying asset. It indicates how much the price of an option is expected to change for a 1% change in implied volatility.

For both call and put options, vega is positive. This implies that as volatility increases, the price of the option generally increases. This is because higher volatility increases the probability of the option finishing in-the-money, thereby increasing its value.

Vega is maximum when the option is ATM and has an intrinsic value of 0.

Options with longer expiration dates generally have higher Vega, as they are more sensitive to changes in volatility.

Mathematically, vega is represented as:

$$v = \frac{\partial C}{\partial \sigma}$$

where:
- C represents the price of the option (or P for the put option).
- σ is the volatility of the underlying asset.

In the context of the Black-Scholes option pricing model, the formula for vega is:

$$v = S * \sqrt{T} * N'(d_1)$$

where:
- S is the current price of the underlying asset.
- T is the time to maturity of the option (in years).
- $N'(d_1)$ is the probability density function (PDF) of the standard normal distribution, and is calculated as:

$$N'(d_1) = \frac{1}{\sqrt{2\pi}} e^{-\frac{d_1^2}{2}}$$

- d_1 is given by:

$$d_1 = \frac{\ln(\frac{S}{K}) + (r + \frac{\sigma^2}{2})T}{\sigma\sqrt{T}}$$

where:
- K is the strike price of the option.
- r is the risk-free interest rate.

- σ is the volatility of the underlying asset.

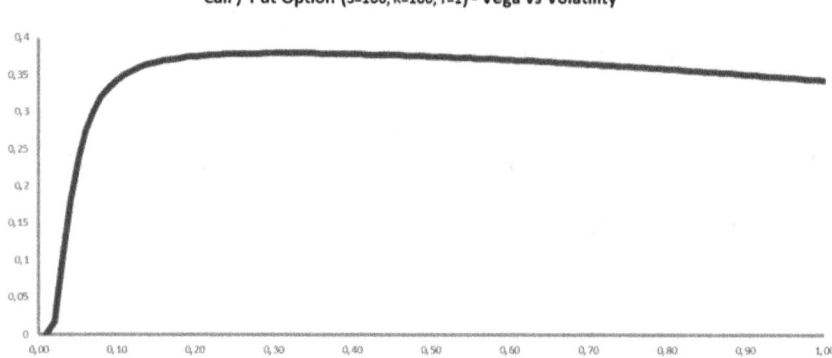

Figure 10 - Call/Put Option - Vega vs Volatility

Suppose you own a call option on Company DEF with a Vega of 0.08.

- **If the implied volatility increases by 1%**, the price of the call option is expected to increase by approximately $0.08.

- **If the implied volatility decreases by 1%**, the price of the call option is expected to decrease by approximately $0.08.

1.4.5 Rho

Rho measures the sensitivity of an option's price to changes in interest rates. It indicates how much the price of an option is expected to change for a 1% change in interest rates.

For a call option, rho is positive. This implies that as the risk-free interest rate increases, the price of the call option tends to increase. This is because a higher interest rate increases the present value of the strike price (which is paid in the future), thereby making the call option more valuable.

For a put option, rho is negative. This indicates that as the risk-free interest rate rises, the price of the put option tends to decrease. This occurs because a higher interest rate reduces the present value of the strike price (which is received in the future), thus reducing the value of the put option.

Rho is generally more significant for options with longer expiration dates and for deep in-the-money options.

Mathematically, rho is defined as:

$$\rho = \frac{\partial C}{\partial r}$$

where:
- C represents the price of the option (or P for the put option).
- r is the risk-free interest rate.

In the context of the Black-Scholes option pricing model, the formula for rho is computed as described below.

For a call option:

$$\rho_{call} = KTe^{-rT}N(d_2)$$

For a put option:

$$\rho_{put} = -KTe^{-rT}N(-d_2)$$

Where:
- T is the time to expiration of the option.
- K is the strike price of the option.
- N(·) is the cumulative distribution function (CDF) of the standard normal distribution.
- d_2 is given by:

$$d_2 = \frac{\ln(\frac{S}{K}) + (r - \frac{\sigma^2}{2})T}{\sigma\sqrt{T}}$$

where:
- S is the current price of the underlying asset.
- σ is the volatility of the underlying asset.

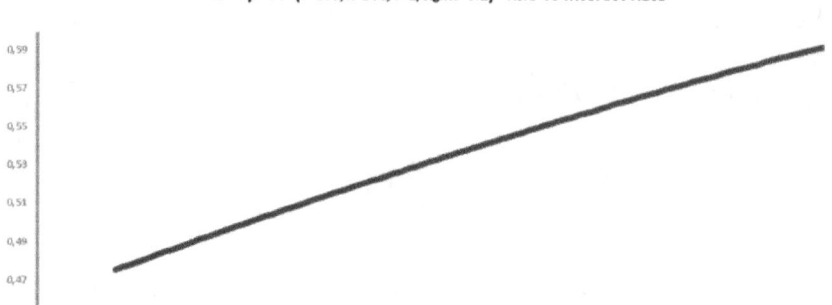

Figure 11 - Call Option - Rho vs Interest Rate

Suppose you own a call option on Company GHI with a Rho of 0.05.

- **If interest rates increase by 1%**, the price of the call option is expected to increase by approximately $0.05.

- **If interest rates decrease by 1%**, the price of the call option is expected to decrease by approximately $0.05.

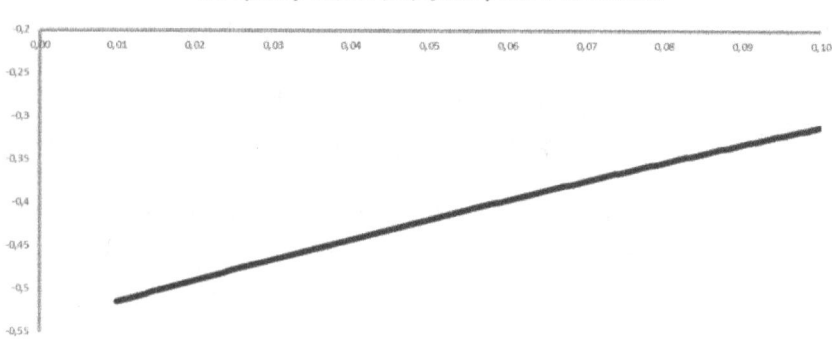

Figure 12 - Put Option - Rho vs Interest Rate

1.4.6 Practical Applications of the Greeks

Understanding the Greeks is essential for effective options trading. Here are some practical applications:

- **Hedging**: By using Delta, traders can hedge their options positions to reduce risk. For example, if you have a portfolio with a high Delta exposure, you might buy or sell options to balance the Delta and mitigate potential losses.

- **Adjusting Positions**: Gamma helps traders understand how Delta will change, allowing them to anticipate and adjust their positions accordingly. High Gamma can indicate increased risk, prompting traders to make adjustments to manage their exposure.

- **Time Decay Management**: Theta helps traders understand the impact of time decay on their options. If you have a short-term options strategy, monitoring Theta is crucial to managing potential losses due to time decay.

- **Volatility Strategies**: Vega is essential for traders who employ volatility strategies. Understanding Vega allows traders to anticipate how changes in volatility will affect their options and adjust their positions to capitalize on or hedge against volatility changes.

- **Interest Rate Considerations**: While Rho is generally less impactful than the other Greeks, it can be important for long-term options and in environments where interest rates are expected to change significantly.

1.5 Practical Advice for Beginners

- **Start Small**: Begin with a small investment and simple strategies like covered calls and cash-secured puts to build confidence and experience.

- **Educate Yourself**: Continuously learn through books, online courses, and webinars. Knowledge is your most valuable asset in options trading.

- **Practice Discipline**: Develop a trading plan and stick to it. Avoid emotional decisions and stay committed to your strategies.

- **Manage Risk**: Always be aware of the risks involved and use risk management techniques to protect your investments.

1.6 Conclusion

By the end of this chapter, you will have a comprehensive understanding of the basics of options trading. This knowledge will serve as the foundation for the more advanced strategies and techniques discussed in subsequent chapters. With a clear grasp of these fundamental concepts, you'll be well-equipped to navigate the options market and begin your journey toward generating consistent income through options trading.

CHAPTER 2

VOLATILITY AND OPTIONS: UNDERSTANDING THE RELATIONSHIP AND STRATEGIES

Volatility is a fundamental concept in options trading, influencing the pricing and behavior of options contracts. Understanding volatility and its implications can provide traders with a significant edge in the market. This chapter delves into the intricacies of volatility, including historical volatility, implied volatility, and the mean-reverting nature of volatility. We will also explore how to compute these metrics and use them to your advantage when trading options.

2.1 Historical Volatility

Historical volatility (HV) measures the actual price fluctuations of an asset over a specific period. It is a statistical measure that reflects the asset's past price movements and is usually expressed as an annualized percentage. HV is calculated using standard deviation, which quantifies the dispersion of returns around the mean.

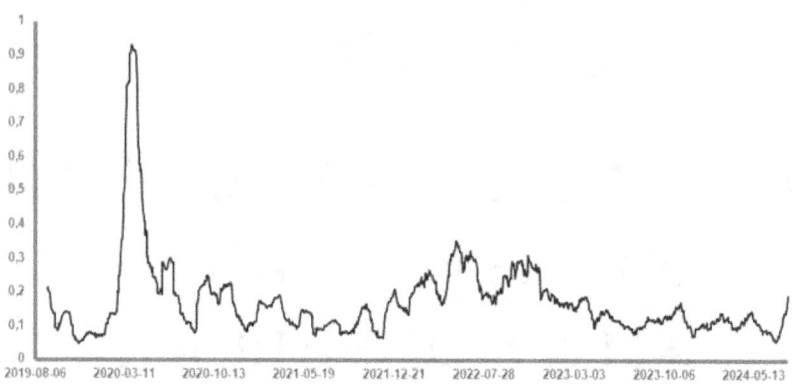

Figure 13 - SPY - Historical Volatility

Steps to Compute Historical Volatility:

- **Collect Price Data**: Gather historical price data for the asset over the desired period.

- **Calculate Daily Returns**: Compute the daily returns by taking the natural logarithm of the price ratio for each consecutive day.

$$\text{Daily Return} = lnP_t - lnP_{t-1}$$

- **Determine the Mean Return**: Calculate the average of the daily returns.

- **Calculate Variance**: Subtract the mean return from each daily return, square the result, and average these squared differences.

$$\text{Variance} = \frac{1}{n-1}\sum_{i=1}^{n}(Daily\ Return_i - Mean\ Return)^2$$

- **Compute Standard Deviation**: Take the square root of the variance to obtain the standard deviation.

- **Annualize Volatility**: Multiply the standard deviation by the square root of the number of trading days in a year (typically 252)

$$\text{Annualized HV} = \sigma * \sqrt{252}$$

Case Study: Historical Volatility of Microsoft (MSFT)

Let's consider Microsoft's (MSFT) stock to illustrate the calculation of historical volatility. Assume we have collected daily closing prices for MSFT over the past 30 trading days.

1. **Daily Returns**
    - If the closing price on day 1 was $300 and on day 2 it was $305, the daily return is: $ln305 - ln300 = 0.0164$

2. **Mean Return**
    - Calculate the average of these daily returns.

3. **Variance and Standard Deviation**
    - Determine the variance by averaging the squared differences from the mean return.
    - Compute the standard deviation (square root of variance).

4. **Annualized Volatility**
    - If the standard deviation of daily returns is 0.02, the annualized historical volatility is: $0.02 * \sqrt{252} = 0.32 = 32\%$

2.2 Implied Volatility

Implied volatility (IV) reflects the market's expectations of future price fluctuations and is derived from the prices of options. Unlike historical volatility, which looks at past price movements, IV is forward-looking and indicates the market's consensus on how volatile the asset will be during the life of the option.

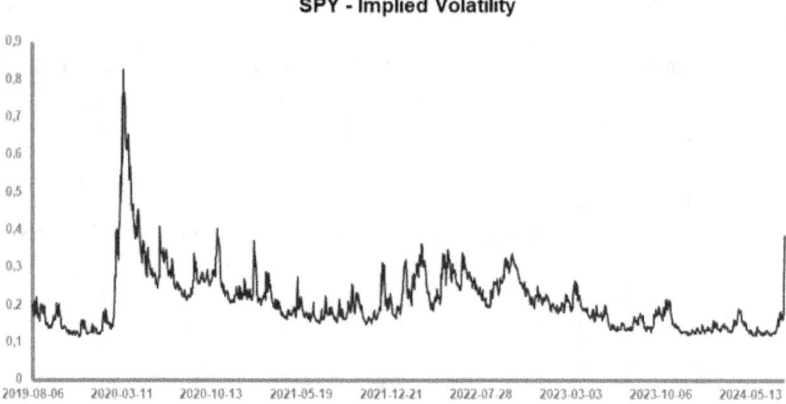

Figure 14 - SPY - Implied Volatility

IV is not directly observable and must be extracted from the prices of options using models like the Black-Scholes model (see Annex). The process involves inputting the current option price, underlying asset price, strike price, risk-free rate, and time to expiration into the model and solving for the volatility component.

Case Study: Implied Volatility of Microsoft (MSFT)

Suppose a Microsoft (MSFT) call option with a strike price of $340, expiring in 30 days, is trading at $7. Using the Black-Scholes model with the following inputs:

- **Current Price:** $340
- **Strike Price:** $340
- **Time to Expiration:** 30 days
- **Risk-Free Rate:** 2%
- **Option Price:** $7

By solving the Black-Scholes equation for volatility, we might find that the implied volatility is 25%.

2.3 Comparing Historical and Implied Volatility

Historical volatility provides insights into how volatile an asset has been, while implied volatility indicates market expectations of future volatility. Comparing HV and IV can reveal valuable trading opportunities.

- **When IV > HV:**
    - This suggests that the market expects higher volatility in the future than what has been observed historically. Options may be overpriced, presenting an opportunity to sell options.

- **When IV < HV:**
    - This indicates that the market expects lower future volatility. Options might be underpriced, making buying options potentially profitable.

Exploiting High Implied Volatility:

High implied volatility often results in higher option premiums. Selling options in a high IV environment can be advantageous because:

- **Higher Premiums:** Generate more income from selling options.
- **Mean Reversion:** Volatility tends to revert to its mean, and high IV usually decreases over time, reducing the risk of significant price swings.

Example: Assume ABC's historical volatility is 20%, but current implied volatility is 30%. Selling a call option with a strike price of $350, expiring in 30 days, could yield a premium of $10 instead of the usual $7 due to the inflated IV.

2.4 Mean-Reverting Nature of Volatility

Volatility exhibits mean-reverting behavior, meaning it tends to fluctuate around a long-term average. Extreme levels of volatility, whether high or low, are typically unsustainable and revert to the mean over time.

Understanding mean reversion helps traders anticipate changes in volatility and adjust their strategies accordingly. For instance, after a period of high volatility (i.e. high premiums), traders might expect a volatility reduction and position themselves to gain from premium reduction.

Example: Consider the S&P 500 Index, which historically has a volatility range between 10% and 25%. During a sell-off market phase, the volatility might spike to 30%. A trader anticipating a return to the mean might position to exploit the expected volatility reduction, expecting lower option premiums as a result. In this situation, selling option can be a valuable strategy, since the option prices are exceptionally high due to the market situation.

Case Study: Selling Covered Calls in High IV Environment

Setup:

- **Stock:** MSFT
- **Current Price:** $340
- **High IV:** 30% (compared to 20% IV)
- **Strike Price:** $350
- **Premium:** $10

Outcome:

- **Premium Collected:** $1,000 for 1 contract (100 shares)
- **If Stock Stays Below $350:** Keep the premium and potentially repeat the process
- **If Stock Exceeds $350:** Stock is called away, but the trader still profits from the premium and capital gain

Case Study: Selling Cash-Secured Puts in High IV Environment

Setup:

- **Stock:** MSFT
- **Current Price:** $340
- **High IV:** 30% (compared to 20% IV)
- **Strike Price:** $330

- **Premium:** $10

Outcome:

- **Premium Collected:** $1,000 for 1 contract (100 shares)
- **If Stock Stays Below $330:** Keep the premium and potentially repeat the process
- **If Stock Exceeds $330:** Buy the stock at an effective cost basis of $320 (strike price – premium)

2.5 IMPLIED VOLATILITY RANK AND PERCENTILE

Implied volatility (IV) is a crucial concept in options trading, reflecting the market's expectations of future price fluctuations of an underlying asset. However, to effectively utilize IV in trading strategies, it's essential to understand and apply metrics like Implied Volatility Rank (IV Rank) and Implied Volatility Percentile (IV Percentile). These metrics provide insights into whether the current IV is high or low relative to historical levels, helping traders make informed decisions.

2.5.1 Implied Volatility Rank (IV Rank)

IV Rank measures the current level of implied volatility compared to its range over a specified period, typically the past year. It indicates where the current IV stands relative to the highest and lowest IV values during that period.

$$\text{IV Rank} = \frac{IV_{current} - IV_{low}}{IV_{high} - IV_{low}} * 100$$

- IV Current: Current implied volatility

- IV Low: Lowest implied volatility in the past year

- IV High: Highest implied volatility in the past year

Interpretation:

- **IV Rank of 100:** Current IV is at its highest point in the past year.

- **IV Rank of 0:** Current IV is at its lowest point in the past year.
- **IV Rank of 50:** Current IV is in the middle of its one-year range.

Case Study: SPY ETF

Setup:

- Stock: SPY
- IV Current: 20%
- IV Low (past year): 10%
- IV High (past year): 30%

Result:

- IV Rank: $\frac{IV_{current} - IV_{low}}{IV_{high} - IV_{low}} * 100 = \frac{20\% - 10\%}{30\% - 10\%} * 100 = 50$

An IV Rank of 50 suggests that the current IV is exactly in the middle of its range over the past year.

Traders often prefer to sell options when IV Rank is high (e.g., above 50) because options premiums are higher, potentially leading to more significant income from option selling strategies like covered calls or cash-secured puts.

2.5.2 Implied Volatility Percentile (IV Percentile)

IV Percentile measures the percentage of days over a specified period (usually the past year) that the implied volatility was lower than the current level. It provides a broader context by comparing the current IV to the distribution of past IV values.

- **IV Percentile of 90:** Current IV is higher than 90% of the days in the past year.
- **IV Percentile of 10:** Current IV is higher than only 10% of the days in the past year.

Case Study: SPY ETF

Consider the SPY ETF with the following daily IV data for the past year:

- 20% of the days had an IV lower than 15%
- 50% of the days had an IV lower than 20%
- 30% of the days had an IV lower than 25%

If the current IV is 20%, the IV Percentile would be 50, indicating that the current IV is higher than 50% of the days in the past year.

High IV Percentile (e.g., above 80) signals that the current IV is relatively high compared to the past year, suggesting it might be a good time to sell options.

2.5.3 Combining IV Rank and IV Percentile for Trading Decisions

Using IV Rank and IV Percentile together provides a more comprehensive view of the current IV environment. Here's how you can integrate both into your trading strategy:

- **High IV Rank and High IV Percentile:**
    - Indicates that IV is high relative to its historical range and most days in the past year.
    - **Strategy:** Favor selling options (e.g., covered calls, cash-secured puts) to capitalize on higher premiums.

- **Low IV Rank and Low IV Percentile:**
    - Indicates that IV is low relative to its historical range and most days in the past year.
    - **Strategy:** Favor buying options (e.g., long calls, long puts) to benefit from potential increases in IV.

- **Mixed Signals:**
    - If IV Rank is high but IV Percentile is low (or vice versa), consider additional factors such as overall market conditions, upcoming events, and personal risk tolerance before making a decision.

Case Study: SPY ETF

Imagine you are considering trading options on the SPY ETF. Here's how you might apply IV Rank and IV Percentile

- **Calculate IV Rank and IV Percentile:**
    - Suppose the current IV of SPY is 25%
    - Over the past year, the lowest IV was 15% and the highest was 35%
    - IV Rank = 50
    - Historical data shows that 70% of the time, IV was below 25%
    - IV Percentile = 70

- **Interpret the data:**
    - An IV Rank of 50 indicates that the current IV is in the middle of its historical range
    - An IV Percentile of 70 indicates that the current IV is higher than 70% of the days in the past year

- **Make a Trading Decision:**
    - The mixed signal suggests a balanced approach
    - Option Selling Strategy: If you lean towards selling, consider selling options because the IV is relatively high compared to most days
    - Option Buying Strategy: If you lean towards buying, the decision is less clear, but you might wait for a lower IV Percentile or look for other confirming indicators

2.6 VOLATILITY SKEW

Volatility skew, or volatility smile, represents the variation in implied volatility across options with different strike prices and maturities. This phenomenon is critical in options pricing and trading as it reflects market participants' perceptions of risk and future volatility. For option income strategies such as covered calls and cash-secured puts, understanding volatility skew is essential for optimizing trade decisions and managing risk. This chapter explores the concept of volatility skew, its significance, methods for computation, and its implications for option income strategies.

2.6.1 Defining Volatility Skew

Volatility skew refers to the pattern of implied volatility (IV) variations for options with different strike prices but the same expiration date. Unlike the Black-Scholes model's assumption of constant volatility, real markets exhibit skewed volatility profiles. There are three primary types of volatility skew:

- **Vertical Skew:** Variation in implied volatility for options with different strike prices but the same expiration date.

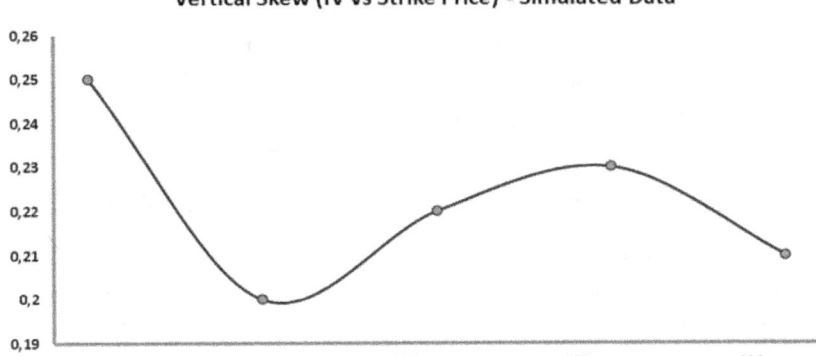

Figure 15 - Vertical Skew (IV vs Strike Price) - Simulated Data

- **Horizontal Skew:** Variation in implied volatility for options with different expiration dates but the same strike price.

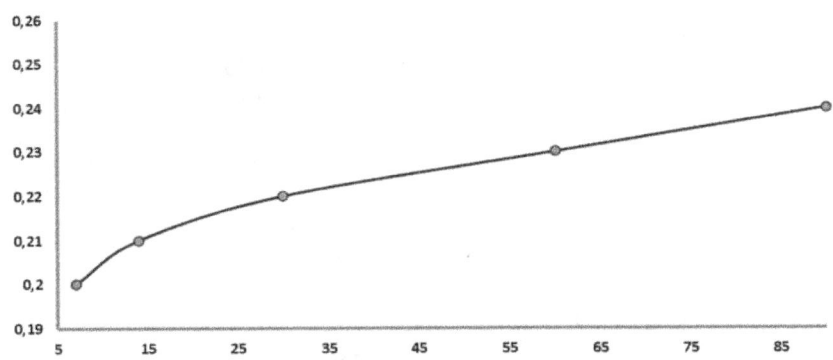

Figure 16 - Horizontal Skew (IV vs Days to Expiration) - Simulated Data

- **Smirk or Smile:** Terms often used to describe the shape of the volatility skew curve, where implied volatility may be higher for deep in-the-money or out-of-the-money options compared to at-the-money options.

Volatility skew provides insights into market sentiment, risk perception, and potential price movements. It reflects the market's expectations of future volatility and can indicate investor concerns about tail risks or extreme price movements. Understanding volatility skew is crucial for:

- **Pricing Accuracy:** Accurate pricing of options requires adjustments for volatility skew rather than relying on constant volatility assumptions.
- **Risk Management:** Helps in assessing potential risk exposure and making informed decisions on option selection.
- **Strategy Optimization:** Influences the selection of strike prices and expiration dates for income strategies.

Implied volatility for each option is derived from option pricing models like the Black-Scholes model.

In the presence of a volatility skew, selecting strike prices outside of the typical at-the-money range may result in more favorable premiums. However, it is important to balance higher premiums against the risk of price movements.

2.6.2 Quantitative Techniques for Analyzing Volatility Skew

Below some of the most used techniques to assess and analyze the volatility skew:

- **Statistical Measures**
  - **Standard Deviation:** Measure the dispersion of implied volatility data from the mean to understand the extent of skew.
  - **Regression Analysis:** Perform regression analysis of implied volatility against strike prices to quantify the nature of the skew and predict future movements.

- **Modeling Volatility Surface**
  - **Volatility Surface:** Construct a 3D model plotting implied volatility against both strike prices and expiration dates to gain insights into horizontal and vertical skew patterns.

Example: Use regression analysis to model the relationship between implied volatility and strike price. A quadratic regression model might fit the skew pattern, providing a quantitative basis for predicting future skew changes and optimizing option strategies.

2.7 Volatility Surface

The volatility surface is a critical concept in options trading, providing a comprehensive view of how implied volatility varies with different strike prices and maturities. Understanding the volatility surface is essential for traders and investors, particularly when employing option income strategies such as covered calls and cash-secured puts. This chapter explores the volatility surface in detail, including its definition, significance, methods of computation, and implications for option income strategies.

2.7.1 Defining Volatility Surface

The volatility surface is a three-dimensional graphical representation of implied volatility across various strike prices and expiration dates. It reflects the market's expectations of future volatility for different options and is typically plotted with strike price on the x-axis, time to maturity on the y-axis, and implied volatility on the z-axis.

- **Market Expectations:** The volatility surface encapsulates market expectations about future volatility, which is crucial for pricing and trading options. It helps traders gauge the market's sentiment and forecast potential price movements.
- **Pricing Accuracy:** By providing a detailed view of implied volatility across different strike prices and maturities, the volatility surface enhances the accuracy of option pricing models. It enables traders to make informed decisions regarding the fair value of options.
- **Risk Management:** Understanding the volatility surface aids in assessing the risk associated with different options. Traders can identify areas of high or low volatility, which helps in devising strategies that align with their risk tolerance and market outlook.

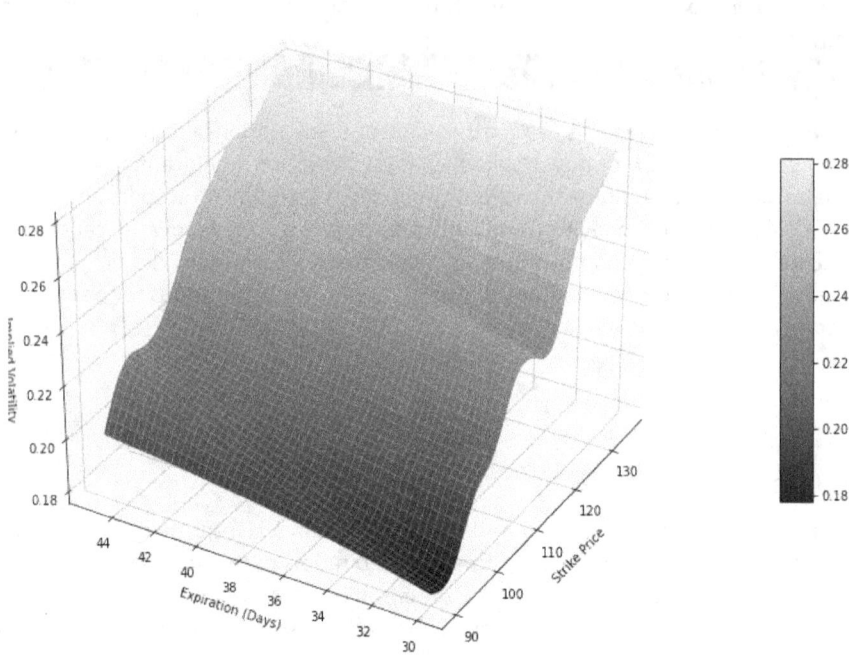

Figure 17 - Volatility Surface

Implied volatility for each option is derived from option pricing models like the Black-Scholes model.

The volatility surface helps in assessing the premiums associated with different strike prices and expiration dates. Higher implied volatility generally translates to higher option premiums, enhancing the income potential from selling options. By analyzing the volatility surface, traders can select strike prices where the volatility is relatively high, thereby maximizing the premium received.

2.6 Conclusion

Volatility is a crucial aspect of options trading, influencing both the pricing and strategy decisions. By understanding and analyzing historical and implied volatility, traders can make informed decisions, exploit market inefficiencies, and optimize their strategies for better returns. This chapter has highlighted the significance of volatility, provided methods to compute it, and demonstrated how to use it effectively in options trading. Whether through selling options in a high implied volatility environment or leveraging the mean-reverting nature of volatility, traders can enhance their performance and achieve consistent income.

CHAPTER 3

THE FUNDAMENTAL OF OPTION INCOME STRATEGIES

The purpose of this chapter is to introduce you to the foundational concepts of generating income through options trading. By understanding the fundamentals, you will be equipped with the knowledge needed to execute basic income strategies, manage risk, and maximize returns. We'll delve into the benefits and risks of using options for income, explore key strategies such as covered calls and cash-secured puts, and highlight the importance of selecting the right stocks and options. Real-life examples will provide practical insights, helping you grasp how these strategies work in real market conditions.

3.1 THE CONCEPT OF OPTION INCOME STRATEGIES

Option income strategies involve using options to create regular income. Unlike speculative strategies that rely on predicting market movements, income strategies focus on generating returns through premiums collected by selling options. These strategies can be particularly attractive because they can produce income in various market conditions — whether the market is rising, falling, or moving sideways.

3.2 OVERVIEW OF INCOME STRATEGIES

The next chapters will provide deep insight into the world of option income strategies, here below just a quick overview of the main / most common ones (which will be further detailed in the dedicated sections): Covered Calls and Cash-Secured Puts.

3.2.1 Covered Calls

A covered call strategy involves holding a long position in a stock and selling call options on that same stock. This strategy is often employed when you expect the stock price to remain relatively stable or increase slightly. The income is generated from the premiums received for selling the call options.

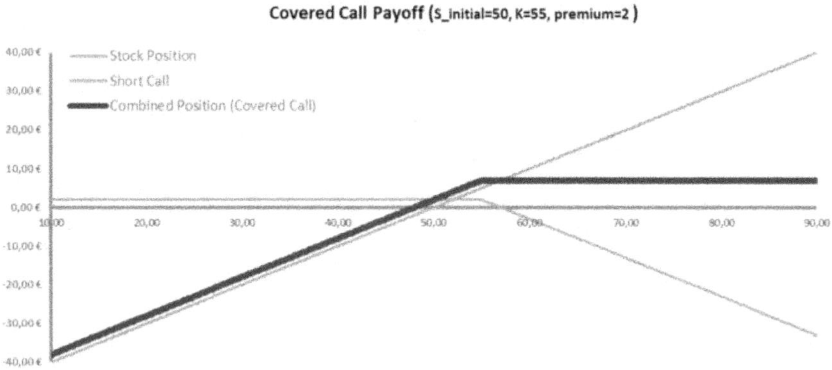

Figure 18 - Covered Call Payoff

Example: let's consider you own 100 shares of XYZ Corporation, currently trading at $50 per share. You decide to sell a call option with a strike price of $55, expiring in one month, for a premium of $2 per share. Here's how this strategy works:

- **Income Generation**: By selling the call option, you receive $200 (100 shares x $2 premium).

- **Possible Outcomes**:
    - If XYZ Corporation's stock price remains below $55, the call option will expire worthless, and you keep the $200 premium as income.
    - If XYZ Corporation's stock price exceeds $55, the buyer of the call option will exercise their

right to purchase the shares at $55. You still keep the $200 premium, and you also gain from selling the stock at $55, resulting in a total return of $700 ($500 from stock price increase + $200 premium).

3.2.2 Cash-Secured Puts

A cash-secured put strategy involves selling put options while holding enough cash to purchase the underlying stock if the option is exercised. This strategy is useful when you are willing to buy the stock at a lower price and want to generate income while waiting for the price to drop.

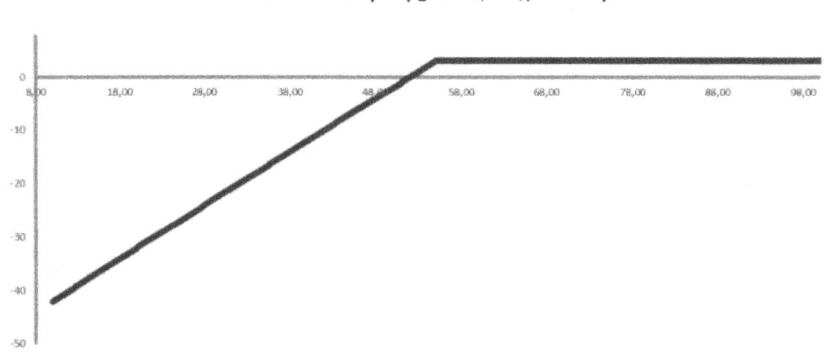

Figure 19 - Cash-Secured Put Payoff

Example: suppose you are interested in buying shares of ABC Corporation, currently trading at $60 per share. You sell a put option with a strike price of $55, expiring in one month, for a premium of $3 per share. Here's how this strategy works:

- **Income Generation**: By selling the put option, you receive $300 (100 shares x $3 premium).

- **Possible Outcomes**:

    - If ABC Corporation's stock price remains above $55, the put option will expire worthless, and you keep the $300 premium as income.

- If ABC Corporation's stock price falls below $55, you will be obligated to buy the stock at $55. You still keep the $300 premium, effectively reducing your purchase price to $52 per share ($55 strike price - $3 premium).

3.3 BENEFITS AND RISKS OF USING OPTIONS FOR INCOME

3.3.1 Benefits

- **Additional Income**: Selling options generates premium income, providing an additional revenue stream on top of potential stock gains or dividends.

- **Flexibility**: Options strategies can be tailored to suit different market conditions and investment goals, allowing for greater flexibility in portfolio management.

- **Risk Management**: Strategies like covered calls can reduce downside risk by providing a buffer against minor stock declines through the premiums received.

3.3.2 Risks

- **Limited Upside Potential**: With covered calls, if the stock price rises significantly above the strike price, you miss out on potential gains beyond the strike price.

- **Obligation to Buy or Sell**: Selling options obligates you to buy or sell the underlying stock if the option is exercised, which may not always align with your investment goals.

- **Market Volatility**: Options prices are influenced by market volatility, which can lead to unpredictable outcomes and potential losses if not managed carefully.

3.4 STATISTICAL EDGE

Selling options for income leverages the inherent advantages of option pricing dynamics, providing an edge that, when managed effectively, can lead to sustained profitability.

3.4.1 Understanding the Edge in Option Selling

At the core of options trading lies the concept of option pricing, governed by models such as the Black-Scholes model (see Annex). When selling options, traders capitalize on the decay of the option's extrinsic value over time, commonly referred to as "theta decay." This decay accelerates as the option approaches its expiration date, providing the option seller with a steady stream of potential income.

From a probabilistic standpoint, selling options, particularly those out-of-the-money (OTM), can be advantageous due to the statistical likelihood of these options expiring worthless. The seller collects the premium upfront, and if the option expires without being exercised, the entire premium is retained as profit. The strategy's edge comes from the fact that the market often overestimates the probability of significant price movements, leading to inflated option premiums. Sellers benefit from this overestimation by consistently capturing these premiums.

Mathematically, the profitability of selling options can be analyzed using the concept of expected value (EV) (for additional insight into the topic, see *The Option Trader's Income Blueprint: Strategic Adjustments and Quantitative Risk Management*, the dedicated volume of this series). For an option seller, the expected value is:

$$EV = P(expire\ worthless) * Premium - P(in\ the\ money) * Loss$$

Where:
- P(expire worthless) is the probability that the option expires worthless.
- P(in the money) is the probability that the option is exercised.

Given that most options, particularly OTM options, tend to expire worthless, the expected value for option sellers is often positive, providing a statistical edge over time.

3.4.2 The Role of Implied and Historical Volatility

As described in the previous chapters, volatility is a critical factor in option pricing. Implied volatility (IV) represents the market's expectations of future volatility and is embedded in the option's premium. Historical volatility (HV), on the other hand, measures the actual past price fluctuations of the underlying asset.

The edge in selling options is often more pronounced in environments where IV is elevated compared to HV. High implied volatility typically inflates option premiums, providing sellers with more substantial income opportunities. When IV is high relative to HV, the market is anticipating more significant price swings than have historically occurred, often leading to overpriced options. Selling options in such conditions can be highly profitable, as the likelihood of the underlying asset moving enough to make the option profitable for the buyer decreases.

Example: Suppose an investor sells a 30-day out-of-the-money (OTM) call option on a stock with an implied volatility of 25%. If the realized volatility over the next 30 days turns out to be 20%, the seller benefits from the volatility premium. If the option was sold for $2.00, and due to the lower realized volatility, its value drops to $1.00, the seller captures a profit of $1.00 per option.

A trader can rely on the concepts of Implied Volatility Rank (IVR) and Implied Volatility Percentile (IVP) described in the previous chapters to assess whether implied volatility is high or low relative to its historical values.

Optimal Market Environment:

- **High IVR/IVP**: When the implied volatility rank or percentile is high, it suggests that options are relatively expensive. This scenario presents a favorable environment for selling options as the premiums collected are likely to be higher, offering more income potential.

- **Decreasing IV**: A market where implied volatility is expected to decrease is ideal for option sellers. As IV drops, the extrinsic value of the option decreases, allowing sellers to buy back the option at a lower price or let it expire worthless, thus locking in profits.

Conversely, in low-volatility environments, option premiums are typically lower, reducing the income potential from selling options. Traders need to be cautious in such conditions, as the lower premiums may not adequately compensate for the risk taken.

3.4.3 The Role of Systematic Trading and Adjustments

The effectiveness and sustainability of the option income strategies depend significantly on systematic trading and timely adjustments. These components play a crucial role in ensuring profitability and maintaining alignment with evolving market conditions.

- **Systematic Trading and Risk Management**: Systematic trading involves employing a predefined set of rules to execute trading strategies consistently.

    Consistency and a systematic approach enhance profitability by minimizing emotional biases and ensuring disciplined execution of trading strategies.

    It is a key component to make the statistical edge work in the long term.

    The same applies to risk management (as described in the dedicated volume: *The Option Trader's Income Blueprint: Strategic Adjustments and Quantitative Risk Management*), in order to always ensure that the trader monitors the positions and applies strict position sizing and diversification in order to preserve capital and keep the risk under control.

- **Role of Adjustments in Maintaining Strategy Alignment**: Adjustments are crucial in aligning an option income strategy with current market conditions (they will be thoroughly described in the next chapters and in the other two volumes of the series: *The Option Trader's Income Blueprint: Strategic Adjustments and Quantitative Risk Management* and *The Option Trader's Income Blueprint: Unleash the Power of Advanced Income Strategies*). They involve modifying the position in response to changes in the underlying asset's price, implied volatility, or other market factors.

    Adjustments help manage risk and optimize the strategy's performance in order to keep the EV profitable.

    Adjustments ensure that the option position remains within a favorable risk-reward profile.

3.5 Conclusion

By understanding and implementing these basic income strategies, you can enhance your investment portfolio's returns while managing risk effectively.

Selling options for income offers a distinct edge rooted in the probabilistic nature of option pricing and the tendency for options, particularly those that are out-of-the-money, to expire worthless. This edge is enhanced in high implied volatility environments, where inflated premiums provide more substantial income opportunities.

Consistency, a systematic trading and risk management approach and timely adjustments are key components to ensure a positive EV and profitability.

The following chapters will delve deeper into advanced strategies and real-life case studies, providing a comprehensive guide to successful options trading.

CHAPTER 4

STRATEGIC ASSET SELECTION FOR OPTION INCOME STRATEGIES

Option income strategies, such as covered calls and cash-secured puts, require careful asset selection to optimize the balance between risk and reward. Identifying suitable assets involves the application of quantitative techniques that incorporate both technical and fundamental analyses. This chapter provides a comprehensive examination of the quantitative methods used to identify assets that align with the objectives of option income strategies, focusing on volatility, return metrics, liquidity, and fundamental analysis through quantitative lenses.

The chapters will provide multiple techniques for each analysis, the trader can choose among them to select the ones that are more useful / applicable to the specific situation.

When trading and investing, the analysis on the historical data should always be considered a starting point, to be assessed considering also the current economic situation and the future expectations about the specific asset and economic environment.

4.1 UNDERLYING ASSETS FOR OPTION INCOME STRATEGIES

The selection of appropriate underlying assets is crucial for the success of option income strategies such as covered calls and cash-secured puts. The choice of underlying assets affects the risk profile, potential returns, and overall effectiveness of the strategy. This chapter examines different types of underlying assets, including stocks, exchange-traded funds (ETFs), indices, and commodities, providing a detailed analysis of their features, advantages, and disadvantages for option income strategies. Real-world examples are provided to illustrate how these assets can be utilized effectively.

4.1.1 Stocks

Stocks are the most common underlying assets used in option income strategies. They represent ownership in a company and are traded on stock exchanges. The volatility, dividend yield, and market sentiment surrounding a stock significantly impact its suitability for option income strategies.

- **Advantages:**
  - **Liquidity:** Many stocks, especially those of large-cap companies, are highly liquid, which ensures narrow bid-ask spreads for options and facilitates the execution of strategies with minimal slippage.
  - **Volatility:** Stocks typically exhibit sufficient volatility to generate attractive premiums from selling options. Higher volatility stocks can offer higher premiums, enhancing income potential.
  - **Dividend Yield:** Stocks that pay regular dividends can further enhance income, particularly when using covered calls. Dividends provide an additional source of return beyond option premiums.

- **Disadvantages:**
  - **Company-Specific Risk:** Stocks are subject to company-specific risks, such as earnings disappointments, regulatory issues, or management changes, which can lead to significant price fluctuations. This risk can adversely impact option income strategies if the stock moves sharply against the position.
  - **Volatility Risk:** While volatility can increase option premiums, excessive volatility can result in large, unpredictable price movements, increasing the likelihood of unfavorable outcomes, such as assignment in

covered calls or substantial losses in cash-secured puts.

Example: Consider a trader selling covered calls on Apple Inc. (AAPL). As of August 2023, AAPL is a highly liquid stock with a market capitalization exceeding $2 trillion. Its options are actively traded, with narrow bid-ask spreads. AAPL's historical volatility is moderate, and it pays a quarterly dividend, making it attractive for covered calls. However, AAPL's stock price is sensitive to earnings reports and broader market sentiment, which could lead to significant price swings and potential risks in executing the strategy.

4.1.2 Exchange-Traded Funds (ETFs)

ETFs are baskets of securities that track an index, sector, commodity, or other assets. They are traded on stock exchanges and can be an effective underlying asset for option income strategies due to their diversification and risk profile.

- **Advantages:**
  - **Diversification:** ETFs inherently provide diversification by holding multiple assets. This reduces the idiosyncratic risk associated with individual stocks and can lead to more stable price behavior.
  - **Liquidity:** Popular ETFs, such as those tracking major indices (e.g., SPY for the S&P 500), are highly liquid, with narrow bid-ask spreads, making them suitable for option income strategies.
  - **Lower Volatility:** ETFs often exhibit lower volatility than individual stocks due to their diversified holdings. This can make them suitable for conservative strategies aimed at generating steady income with reduced risk.

- **Disadvantages:**
  - **Lower Premiums:** The lower volatility of ETFs compared to individual stocks can result in lower option premiums, potentially reducing income generation from option sales.
  - **Sector or Market Risk:** While ETFs reduce individual stock risk, they are still subject to sector or market risk. For instance, an ETF tracking a specific sector (e.g., technology)

may be highly correlated with that sector's performance, which could impact the effectiveness of option income strategies.

Example: A trader might sell cash-secured puts on the SPDR S&P 500 ETF (SPY). SPY is one of the most liquid ETFs globally, tracking the S&P 500 index. Its options are among the most actively traded, offering narrow bid-ask spreads and deep liquidity. Due to its broad diversification across 500 large-cap U.S. companies, SPY exhibits lower volatility than most individual stocks, making it suitable for conservative option income strategies. However, during market-wide downturns, such as the 2020 COVID-19 crash, SPY experienced significant price declines, which could pose risks to cash-secured put sellers.

4.1.3 Indices

Indices represent the performance of a group of stocks, typically based on specific criteria such as market capitalization, sector, or region. While indices themselves cannot be traded directly, index options and index-tracking ETFs or futures provide a way to use indices as underlying assets in option income strategies.

- **Advantages:**
    - **Broad Market Exposure:** Indices offer exposure to a wide range of stocks, reducing the impact of individual stock movements on the strategy's performance.
    - **Stability:** Due to their diversified nature, indices often exhibit more stable price behavior compared to individual stocks, reducing the risk of significant price swings.
    - **Liquidity:** Index options and ETFs, such as those on the S&P 500 or NASDAQ 100, are highly liquid, facilitating efficient execution of option income strategies.

- **Disadvantages:**
    - **Limited Upside Potential:** The broad exposure and reduced volatility of indices can limit the potential for large premiums compared to more volatile individual stocks.
    - **Correlation with Market Risk:** Indices are inherently correlated with the broader market, meaning they are susceptible to

macroeconomic factors and market-wide events that can impact option strategies.

Example: A trader using the CBOE S&P 500 Index (SPX) options for a covered call strategy might benefit from the index's stability and liquidity. SPX options are European-style and cash-settled, reducing the risk of early assignment. However, because SPX tracks a broad market index, it may offer lower premiums compared to individual high-volatility stocks, and the strategy's performance is closely tied to overall market trends.

4.1.4 Commodities

Commodities, including gold, oil, and agricultural products, can be underlying assets for options through futures contracts or ETFs that track commodity prices. Commodities offer a unique risk-reward profile, driven by factors such as supply-demand dynamics, geopolitical events, and economic indicators.

- **Advantages:**
    - **Diversification:** Commodities often have low correlation with stocks and bonds, providing diversification benefits within an option income portfolio.
    - **High Volatility:** Certain commodities, such as oil, exhibit high price volatility, leading to higher option premiums. This can enhance income generation in option strategies.

- **Disadvantages:**
    - **Complex Pricing Factors:** Commodity prices are influenced by a wide range of factors, including geopolitical events, weather patterns, and global supply-demand dynamics. These complexities can make it challenging to predict price movements and implement effective option income strategies.
    - **Liquidity Issues:** Some commodity options, especially those on less popular commodities, may have lower liquidity compared to stock or index options, leading to wider bid-ask spreads and potential execution challenges.

Example: Consider a trader selling covered calls on the SPDR Gold Shares ETF (GLD), which tracks the price of gold. Gold is often seen as a safe-haven asset, and its price can be highly volatile during periods of economic uncertainty. This volatility can generate attractive premiums for covered calls. However, the trader must be aware of the unique factors influencing gold prices, such as central bank policies, inflation expectations, and geopolitical events, which could impact the effectiveness of the strategy.

4.2 QUANTITATIVE TECHNIQUES FOR VOLATILITY ASSESSMENT

As described in the previous chapter, volatility is a cornerstone of options trading, particularly in income-generating strategies such as covered calls and cash-secured puts. It directly influences the pricing of options and, consequently, the premiums that traders can earn. Understanding and analyzing volatility allows traders to identify optimal assets for these strategies, balancing the potential for income generation with the associated risks.

This chapter will add further details which can help the trader to make informed decisions during the asset selection process.

4.2.1 The Role of Volatility in Option Income Strategies

Volatility represents the degree of variation in the price of a financial asset over time. It is a measure of the uncertainty or risk related to the change in the asset's price. In the context of options, volatility is a critical input for pricing models, as it directly affects the option premium. The greater the expected volatility of the underlying asset, the higher the potential for large price movements, which increases the value of the option.

Option premiums consist of intrinsic value and time value, with volatility playing a key role in determining the time value. Higher volatility increases the time value of the option, as it raises the probability of the option expiring in-the-money (ITM). For option income strategies like covered calls and cash-secured puts, selecting assets with appropriate volatility levels is essential to optimize the income generated through premiums while managing risk.

While higher volatility can lead to higher premiums, it also increases the likelihood of significant adverse price movements in the underlying asset. For instance, in a covered call strategy, if the underlying asset experiences a sharp rise, the option may be exercised, and the asset may be called away, potentially capping the trader's profit. Conversely, in a cash-secured put strategy, a significant drop in the asset's price could result in the trader being assigned the asset at a higher-than-market price. Therefore, understanding and managing volatility is crucial to balance income potential with risk.

4.2.2 Quantitative Techniques for Volatility Assessment

Here below the most used quantitative techniques:

- **Implied Volatility:** reflects the market's expectation of the asset's future volatility. It is derived from the market price of options using models like the Black-Scholes formula. Unlike historical volatility, which is based on past price movements, IV is forward-looking and changes in response to market sentiment and conditions.

  Traders often seek assets with high IV for selling options (see also IV Rank and IV percentile, discussed in the previous chapters), as this results in higher premiums. However, it's crucial to consider the potential risks associated with high IV, as it might indicate that the market expects significant price fluctuations. To optimize income while managing risk, traders should compare IV across various assets to identify those with favorable volatility profiles.

  Example: Suppose a trader is considering selling covered calls on two stocks. Stock A has an IV of 40%, while Stock B has an IV of 25%. The higher IV of Stock A suggests that its options will command a higher premium, making it more attractive for generating income through covered calls. However, the trader must also consider the risk of greater price volatility in Stock A.

- **Historical Volatility:** Historical volatility (HV) measures the actual price movements of an asset over a specific period. It is calculated as the standard deviation of the asset's returns, typically on a daily, weekly, or monthly basis. Historical volatility provides insights into how much the asset's price has fluctuated in the past, offering a baseline for comparison with implied volatility.

  Historical volatility is useful for identifying assets that have exhibited stable price behavior in the past, which may be preferred for strategies aiming to minimize risk. As described in the previous chapters, by comparing HV with IV, traders can assess whether the current market expectations of volatility align with historical trends.

  Example: Consider a stock with an HV of 20% and an IV of 30%. The difference between HV and IV suggests that the market expects future volatility to be higher than what has been observed historically. This discrepancy might indicate a temporary market anomaly or upcoming events that could cause significant price movements. For an income strategy, the trader might favor this stock for selling options due to the higher premiums associated with elevated IV.

- **Importance of the Volatility Ratio:** The volatility ratio, calculated as the ratio of implied volatility to historical volatility (IV/HV), is a critical metric for assessing whether an asset is over- or underpriced in terms of its options. A ratio greater than 1 suggests that the market expects future volatility to exceed past volatility, which can create opportunities for selling options at inflated premiums.

$$\text{Volatility Ratio} = \frac{\text{Implied Volatility (IV)}}{\text{Historical Volatility (HV)}}$$

- **IV/HV > 1:** This scenario suggests that the market expects higher future volatility. Traders can capitalize on this by selling options, anticipating that the volatility might revert to historical norms, leading to the decay of option premiums and profitable option selling.
- **IV/HV < 1:** This condition indicates that the market expects lower future volatility compared to historical levels. In this case, the option premiums might be lower, and the trader should exercise caution or seek assets with a volatility ratio greater than 1.

Example: If Stock X has an IV of 35% and an HV of 25%, the volatility ratio is 1.4, suggesting that the market expects a significant increase in volatility. This higher ratio might make Stock X a candidate for selling covered calls, as the elevated IV could lead to higher premiums. However, the trader must also be prepared for potential volatility spikes.

Additional advanced volatility measures:

- **Beta:** Beta (see Annex) measures an asset's sensitivity to market movements and is often used to assess systemic risk. A beta greater than 1 indicates that the asset is more volatile than the market, while a beta less than 1 suggests lower volatility. Beta can be incorporated into the selection process to ensure that the chosen assets align with the trader's risk tolerance.

- **Volatility Skew:** Volatility skew refers to the difference in implied volatility between out-of-the-money (OTM), at-the-money (ATM), and in-the-money (ITM) options. A steep skew indicates higher demand for OTM options, often due to market fears of large moves. Analyzing skew helps traders understand market sentiment and choose strike prices that maximize premium income while managing risk.

- **Volatility Surface:** The volatility surface plots implied volatility across different strike prices and expiration dates, providing a three-dimensional view of how volatility changes with moneyness and time. By examining the volatility surface, traders can identify optimal strikes and expirations for selling options that offer the best premiums relative to their risk.

Example: If a trader observes that the volatility surface for a particular stock shows a pronounced increase in IV for short-dated OTM options, they might choose to sell covered calls at these strikes to capture higher premiums, while also being cautious of the potential for large price swings.

4.3 RETURN METRICS AND RISK-ADJUSTED PERFORMANCE

In the realm of options trading, selecting assets for income strategies such as covered calls and cash-secured puts necessitates a thorough evaluation of return metrics and risk-adjusted performance. This chapter delves deeper into the quantitative techniques used to assess these aspects, focusing on how they can guide the selection of assets that not only offer potential for income generation but also align with a trader's risk tolerance. Understanding and applying these metrics enable traders to make more informed decisions and improve the likelihood of achieving their financial objectives.

4.3.1 Historical Returns

As anticipated in the previous chapters, historical returns provide a basis for understanding how an asset has performed in the past. This information is crucial for assessing the stability and potential profitability of assets in option income strategies. While past performance does not guarantee future results, a consistent historical return can be indicative of a more predictable and reliable asset.

When selecting assets for option income strategies, analyzing the historical performance involves looking at:

- **Average Annual Return:** Provides an overview of the asset's long-term performance.

- **Return Volatility:** Measures the variability of returns, which impacts the predictability of the asset's performance.

Example: A stock with an average annual return of 8% and a standard deviation of 15% may offer consistent returns but with moderate volatility.

4.3.2 Risk-Adjusted Performance Metrics

Risk-adjusted performance metrics evaluate returns in the context of the risk taken. These metrics are essential for comparing assets with varying levels of volatility and risk, ensuring that returns are considered in light of their associated risks.

- **Sharpe Ratio:** The Sharpe Ratio measures the return earned in excess of the risk-free rate per unit of volatility. It is calculated as:

$$\text{Sharpe Ratio} = \frac{R_p - R_f}{\sigma_p}$$

Where:
- R_p is the portfolio return,
- R_f is the risk-free rate (e.g., the yield on a Treasury bond),
- σ_p is the standard deviation of the portfolio returns.

A higher Sharpe Ratio indicates better risk-adjusted performance, making it an attractive metric for option income strategies (for example for Covered Calls).

Example: If Stock E has an annual return of 12%, a risk-free rate of 2%, and a standard deviation of 10%, the Sharpe Ratio is:

$$\text{Sharpe Ratio} = \frac{12\% - 2\%}{10\%} = 1.0$$

- **Sortino Ratio:** The Sortino Ratio is a variation of the Sharpe Ratio that focuses only on downside risk, which is often more relevant for investors concerned about negative returns (usually it could be useful in case of cash-secured put strategies). It is calculated as:

$$\text{Sortino Ratio} = \frac{R_p - R_f}{\sigma_d}$$

Where σ_d is the standard deviation of negative returns (downside deviation).

Example: If Stock F has a return of 15%, a risk-free rate of 3%, and a downside deviation of 7%, the Sortino Ratio is:

$$\text{Sortino Ratio} = \frac{15\% - 3\%}{7\%} = 1.71$$

- **Alpha:** Alpha (see Annex) measures the excess return of an asset relative to its expected return based on its beta (systematic risk, see

Annex). It indicates the asset's performance relative to a benchmark index.

$$\text{Alpha} = R_p - [R_f + \beta \times (R_m - R_f)]$$

Where:
- R_p is the portfolio return,
- R_f is the risk-free rate,
- β is the asset's beta,
- R_m is the market return.

Example: If Stock G has a return of 14%, a beta of 1.2, the risk-free rate is 2%, and the market return is 10%, the alpha is:

$$\text{Alpha} = 14\% - [2\% + 1.2 \times (10\% - 2\%)] = 14\% - 9.6\% = 4.4\%$$

4.4 LIQUIDITY ANALYSIS

Liquidity is a critical aspect of financial markets, directly impacting the effectiveness of option income strategies such as covered calls and cash-secured puts. Liquidity affects the ease of entering and exiting positions, the cost of trading, and the overall execution quality of options trades. This chapter delves into the quantitative methods for assessing liquidity and how these measures can guide the selection of suitable assets for option income strategies.

Liquidity refers to the ability to quickly buy or sell an asset in the market without causing a significant impact on its price. In the context of options trading, liquidity is crucial for:

- **Minimizing Transaction Costs:** High liquidity generally leads to narrower bid-ask spreads, reducing the cost of entering and exiting trades.
- **Efficient Execution:** Liquidity ensures that trades can be executed promptly and at desired prices, avoiding slippage.
- **Market Stability:** Liquid markets are less prone to dramatic price swings due to large trades, providing a more stable trading environment.

To evaluate liquidity quantitatively, several metrics are employed:

- **Average Daily Volume (ADV):** Measures the average number of shares traded per day over a specific period. Higher ADV indicates greater liquidity.

ADV is calculated by averaging the daily trading volume over a specified period. It can be computed as follows:

$$ADV = \frac{\sum_{i=1}^{N} \text{Volume}_i}{N}$$

Where:
- Volume_i is the trading volume on day i,
- N is the number of days.

- **Bid-Ask Spread:** The difference between the highest price a buyer is willing to pay (bid) and the lowest price a seller will accept (ask). A narrower spread signifies higher liquidity.
- **Open Interest:** Represents the total number of outstanding option contracts that are not yet closed or exercised. Higher open interest indicates stronger market participation and liquidity.

Highly liquid assets should be preferred as underlying assets for option income strategies.

4.5 FUNDAMENTAL ANALYSIS

Fundamental analysis, when coupled with quantitative techniques, offers a robust framework for evaluating the intrinsic value and financial health of potential assets. This chapter delves deeper into advanced fundamental analysis using quantitative methods, focusing on key valuation metrics, financial ratios, and growth indicators that aid in identifying optimal assets for income strategies.

4.5.1 Price-to-Earnings (P/E)

The Price-to-Earnings (P/E) Ratio is a fundamental valuation metric that compares a company's current share price to its earnings per share (EPS). It is calculated as:

$$\text{P/E Ratio} = \frac{\text{Price per Share}}{\text{Earnings per Share}}$$

Interpretations:

- **Valuation Insight:** A lower P/E ratio can indicate that a stock is undervalued relative to its earnings potential, which can be appealing for selling cash-secured puts. Conversely, a high P/E ratio may suggest overvaluation, making the stock less attractive for option strategies.

- **Comparative Analysis:** Comparing the P/E ratio to the industry average and historical P/E of the stock provides context. Stocks with P/E ratios significantly lower than their historical averages or industry peers might be undervalued, presenting opportunities for option strategies.

Example: A company with a current share price of $50 and an EPS of $5 has a P/E ratio of 10. If the industry average P/E ratio is 15, the stock may be undervalued, suggesting it could be a good candidate for cash-secured puts if the fundamentals support a stable or upward price trend.

4.5.2 Price-to-Book (P/B)

The Price-to-Book (P/B) Ratio compares a company's current share price to its book value per share. It is calculated as:

$$\text{P/B Ratio} = \frac{\text{Price per Share}}{\text{Book Value per Share}}$$

Where:

- **Price per Share** is the market price of the stock
- **Book Value per Share** is calculated as:

$$\text{Book Value per Share} = \frac{\text{Total Assets} - \text{Total Liabilities}}{\text{Number of Shares Outstanding}}$$

Interpretations:

- **Valuation Insight:** A P/B ratio below 1 indicates that the stock is trading for less than its book value, suggesting it might be undervalued. This can be particularly relevant for cash-secured puts, as buying undervalued stocks can provide a margin of safety.
- **Asset Quality:** A higher P/B ratio may reflect that the market values the company's intangible assets or growth prospects highly. Analyze the company's asset quality and compare the P/B ratio with industry averages to assess relative valuation.

Example: A stock with a market price of $30 and a book value per share of $25 has a P/B ratio of 1.2. If the industry average P/B ratio is 1.5, the stock may be relatively undervalued. This valuation insight can make it a suitable candidate for cash-secured puts if the fundamentals are strong.

4.5.2 Dividend Yield

The Dividend Yield measures the annual dividend income relative to the stock's price. It is calculated as:

$$\text{Dividend Yield} = \frac{\text{Annual Dividend per Share}}{\text{Price per Share}}$$

Interpretations:

- **Income Generation:** A high dividend yield indicates a higher income return relative to the stock price, which is beneficial for covered calls. Stocks with stable or growing dividends provide additional income, enhancing the appeal of the covered call strategy.
- **Dividend Stability:** Evaluate the history of dividend payments and the company's payout ratio to ensure sustainability. A consistently high dividend yield combined with stable payments suggests financial stability, making the stock a reliable choice for income strategies.

Example: If a stock is trading at 40 with an annual dividend of 2 per share, its dividend yield is 5%. For a covered call strategy, a stock with a 5% yield provides a solid income base, in addition to the premiums earned from selling calls.

4.5.3 Earnings Growth Rate

The Earnings Growth Rate measures the annualized rate at which a company's earnings per share (EPS) have grown over a specified period. It is often calculated using:

$$\text{Earnings Growth Rate} = \frac{(EPS_{current} - EPS_{base})}{EPS_{base}} \times 100$$

Where:

- $EPS_{current}$ is the most recent EPS
- EPS_{base} is the EPS from a previous period

Interpretations:

- **Growth Prospects:** A higher earnings growth rate indicates that the company is expanding its profitability, which can lead to stock price appreciation.

- **Consistency and Sustainability:** Analyze the historical growth rates and future earnings projections. Consistent growth over multiple periods indicates a reliable company with strong future potential.

Example: A company with an EPS growth rate of 10% annually over the past five years suggests robust earnings expansion. This growth potential makes it a strong candidate for covered calls, as the likelihood of significant price appreciation supports higher premiums.

4.5.4 Free Cash Flow

Free Cash Flow (FCF) represents the cash generated by a company after accounting for capital expenditures. It is calculated as:

$$\text{Free Cash Flow} = \text{Operating Cash Flow} - \text{Capital Expenditures}$$

Interpretations:

- **Financial Health:** Positive and growing FCF indicates that the company has ample cash to reinvest in its business, pay dividends, or repurchase shares. This financial flexibility is beneficial for both covered calls and cash-secured puts, as it suggests stability and capacity to manage downturns.
- **Cash Flow Sustainability:** Examine the consistency of FCF over time. Volatile or declining FCF might indicate financial instability, increasing the risk of the underlying stock's price movements.

4.5.5 Debt-to-Equity (D/E)

The Debt-to-Equity (D/E) Ratio measures a company's financial leverage by comparing its total liabilities to shareholders' equity. It is calculated as:

$$\text{Debt-to-Equity Ratio} = \frac{\text{Total Liabilities}}{\text{Shareholders' Equity}}$$

Interpretations:

- **Leverage and Risk:** A lower D/E ratio indicates lower financial leverage and, therefore, less risk associated with the company's

debt obligations. Lower leverage is preferable for income strategies, as it implies greater financial stability.
- **Industry Comparisons:** Compare the D/E ratio to industry averages. Companies with significantly lower D/E ratios than their peers may have a more conservative and safer financial structure.

Example: A company with total liabilities of 400 million and shareholders' equity of 800 million has a D/E ratio of 0.5. This conservative leverage ratio suggests financial stability, making it a more attractive candidate for option income strategies.

4.6 CONCLUSION

Selecting the right asset for option income strategies requires a meticulous evaluation of several key factors. By integrating these elements—volatility, risk-adjusted returns, fundamental ratios, and liquidity—into your asset selection process, you can make informed decisions that enhance the effectiveness of your option income strategies and drive long-term success in your trading endeavors. This comprehensive approach ensures that you not only select assets with favorable characteristics but also align your trading strategy with a well-rounded understanding of the market dynamics.

CHAPTER 5

COVERED CALLS – THE CORNERSTONE OF OPTION INCOME

In the world of options trading, the covered call strategy stands out as one of the most accessible and reliable methods for generating income. This strategy has been a cornerstone of option income for both seasoned investors and newcomers alike. In this chapter, we will delve deeply into the covered call strategy, examining its purpose, execution, and the nuances that make it a preferred choice for many option traders.

To start, let's explore the purpose of this chapter in detail. We aim to demystify the covered call strategy, provide a comprehensive step-by-step guide for implementation, and offer insights into maximizing profits through effective management. By the end of this chapter, you will have a solid understanding of how to use covered calls to enhance your investment income, as well as practical knowledge for selecting stocks and options, managing your trades, and adjusting strategies to fit changing market conditions.

5.1 THE PURPOSE OF COVERED CALLS

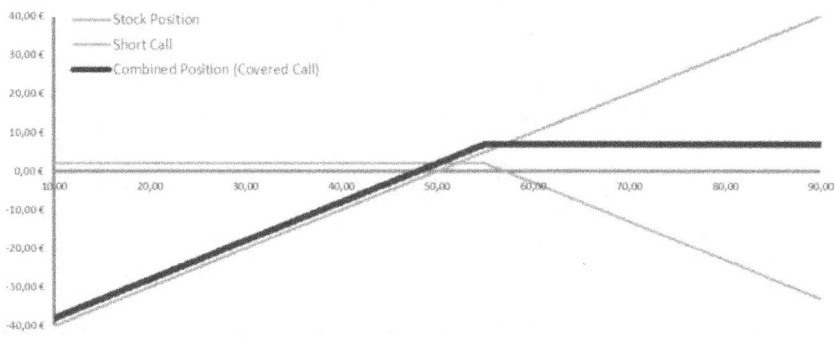

Figure 20 - Covered Call Payoff

The covered call strategy is designed to generate additional income from a stock you already own. It involves selling (or writing) call options against a stock position. This technique is favored for its simplicity and its ability to provide a steady stream of income while managing downside risk.

- **Income Generation:** The primary purpose of a covered call is to generate income. When you sell a call option, you receive a premium from the buyer. This premium is yours to keep, regardless of whether the option is exercised. The income from selling call options can be a valuable supplement to dividends and capital gains.

- **Downside Protection:** While the covered call strategy does not provide full protection against losses, the premium received from selling the call option offers some cushioning. This can offset a portion of any potential declines in the stock's price, reducing the effective loss in a downturn.

- **Enhancing Returns:** For investors who hold stocks that are expected to remain relatively stable or rise slowly, selling covered calls can enhance overall returns. The premium earned from the call options increases the total return on the investment, improving the performance beyond what would be achieved through dividends and stock appreciation.

A covered call includes the following components:

- **Call Option**: A financial contract that gives the buyer the right to buy the underlying stock at the strike price before the option expires.

- **Strike Price**: The price at which you agree to sell the stock if the short call option is exercised.

- **Premium**: The income you receive for selling the call option, which is yours to keep regardless of whether the option is exercised or not.

- **Stock**: The shares of the stock you own. The covered call is sold against them.

5.2 Step-by-Step Guide to Executing a Covered Call

Here's a step-by-step breakdown of how a covered call works:

- **Own the Underlying Stock**: To implement a covered call, you must first own shares of the underlying stock. The number of shares should match the number of contracts you wish to sell, where each options contract typically represents 100 shares..

- **Sell a Call Option**: Choose a call option with a specific strike price and expiration date. The strike price is typically set above the current market price of the stock, reflecting a price at which you are willing to sell the stock if the option is exercised. You then sell the call option, which obligates you to sell your shares at the strike price if the option is exercised before or at expiration.

- **Receive Premium**: Upon selling the call option, you receive a premium, which is the price paid by the option buyer for the right to purchase your shares at the strike price. This premium provides immediate income and is yours to keep, regardless of whether the option is exercised.

- **Hold the Position**: After selling the call, you simply hold the stock and wait for the option to reach its expiration date. During this period, several outcomes are possible depending on the movement of the stock price.

- **Stock Sold (if exercised)**: If the stock price raises above the strike price, the option may be exercised, and you will need to sell the stock at the strike price. However, you keep the premium received from selling the call.

Example: Suppose you own 100 shares of Company XYZ, which is currently trading at $50. You decide to sell a covered call option with a strike price of $55, expiring in one month, and receive a $2 premium per share.

- **Scenario 1**: If XYZ's stock price remains below $55, the call option expires worthless, and you keep the $200 premium as profit.

- **Scenario 2**: If XYZ's stock price rises above $55, the option may be exercised, and you sell 100 shares at $55 each. You still keep the $200 premium.

5.2.1 Choosing the Right Underlying Asset

The first step in executing a covered call strategy is to select the appropriate stock.

Choosing the right stock for a covered call involves evaluating various factors to ensure the strategy's success. Here's a detailed look at how to select suitable stocks:

- **Financial Health and Stability / Stable or Moderate Growth**: Choose stocks with stable or predictable growth. Avoid highly volatile stocks that can experience sharp price swings.
  Choose stocks from companies with strong financials, including consistent revenue growth, profitability, and manageable debt levels. Stocks from well-established, financially stable companies are less likely to experience dramatic price swings.
  Example: Procter & Gamble (PG) is a good candidate due to its consistent performance, solid dividend yield, and stable stock price.

- **Trading Volume and Liquidity**: high liquidity is essential for effective options trading. Stocks with high trading volume ensure that there is sufficient interest in the options market, making it easier to execute trades and manage positions.
  Example: companies like Apple Inc. (AAPL) and Microsoft Corp. (MSFT) are highly liquid, making their options attractive for covered calls.

- **Dividend Yield and Stability**: Stocks that pay dividends can enhance the income potential of your overall investment. A stable dividend yield provides additional income, complementing the premiums earned from covered calls.
  Example: Coca-Cola (KO) offers a reliable dividend yield, which adds to the total return when combined with premiums from selling

covered calls. Coca-Cola's consistent dividend payments enhance the overall income from your investment.

- **Price Volatility**: Opt for stocks with moderate price volatility. While you want some price movement to earn premiums, excessive volatility can lead to unpredictable outcomes and increased risk.
  Example: Walmart (WMT), with its relatively stable price movements, is a suitable candidate for covered calls compared to more volatile stocks like Tesla (TSLA)

For example, consider a well-established company like Johnson & Johnson (JNJ). JNJ has a stable financial history, consistent dividends, and a high trading volume, making it a suitable candidate for covered calls.

Case Study: JNJ Covered Call

Company: Johnson & Johnson (JNJ)

- **Current Stock Price**: $165
- **Dividend Yield**: 2.8%
- **Trading Volume**: High

Strategy:

- **Sell Call Option**: Choose a call option with a strike price of $170 and an expiration date one month away.

Premium Received: $3 per share

Why JNJ?

- **Stability and Growth**: Johnson & Johnson is a well-established company with stable earnings and consistent growth, making it a suitable candidate for covered calls.
- **Liquidity**: JNJ options are highly liquid, with ample open interest and trading volume.
- **Dividend Income**: The dividend yield adds to the overall return on investment, complementing the premium income from the call option.

Potential Outcomes:

- **Stock Price Below $170**: The option expires worthless, and you retain the $3 premium per share, plus any dividends.
- **Stock Price Above $170**: The option is exercised, and you sell your shares at $170, making a capital gain plus the premium received.

5.2.2 Setting Up the Trade

Once you have selected the stock, the next step is to choose the strike price and expiration date for the call option:

- **Strike Price**: The strike price should be higher than the current stock price. This allows you to keep your stock if it does not exceed the strike price by the expiration date.

- **Expiration Date**: Choose an expiration date that aligns with your market outlook and income goals. Shorter expiration periods offer more frequent income opportunities but may provide lower premiums. Longer periods offer potentially higher premiums but less frequent income.

In the covered call strategy, the trade setup is crucial to achieving the desired balance between risk and reward. Two key factors in setting up your covered call trades are **Delta** and **Days to Expiration (DTE)**. Understanding these factors will help you make informed decisions about selecting the right strike prices and expiration dates for your options:

- **Determine Your Income Goals**: Decide how much income you wish to generate and how frequently. Shorter DTE options will allow you to collect premiums more often, while longer DTE options will provide higher premiums but less frequent income.

- **Assess Market Conditions**: Analyze the stock's price movement and volatility. If you expect the stock to remain stable, a lower Delta and longer DTE might be appropriate. If you anticipate price movements, consider higher Delta and shorter DTE options.

- **Select Appropriate Strike Price and Expiration Date**: Based on your analysis, choose a strike price that aligns with your outlook and income goals. Match this with an expiration date that fits your desired income frequency and management preferences.

Here below a detailed description about the rules you might follow to choose delta and DTE for a covered call option strategy:

- **Delta**: As analyzed in the dedicated chapter, Delta is one of the "Greeks" used in options trading to measure the sensitivity of an option's price to changes in the price of the underlying stock. Specifically, Delta represents the amount by which an option's price is expected to change for a one-point change in the underlying stock's price. For covered calls, Delta helps determine how likely an option is to be exercised and how much premium you can earn.

  For call options, Delta ranges from 0 to 1. A Delta of 0.5 means that for every $1 move in the underlying stock, the option's price is expected to move by $0.50. Higher Delta values indicate a higher likelihood that the option will be in the money (i.e., exercised).

  Example: If you are considering selling a call option with a Delta of 0.30 on Microsoft Corporation (MSFT) stock, and MSFT's price rises by $1, the price of the call option would increase by approximately $0.30. This lower Delta suggests a lower probability that the option will be exercised compared to a call option with a Delta closer to 1.

  When selecting the strike price for a covered call, consider the Delta of the call options:

    - **Lower Delta (0.20 - 0.40)**: Selling options with lower Delta values means choosing strike prices further above the current stock price. These options have a lower probability of being exercised, which is ideal if you want to retain your stock and collect premiums without expecting the stock price to rise significantly.

      Example: If MSFT is trading at $320, and you sell a call option with a Delta of 0.35 with a $330 strike price, you are choosing a strike price that is 10 points above the current stock price. The lower Delta indicates a lower probability that MSFT will exceed $330 by the expiration date, meaning you are less likely to have to sell your shares.

    - **Higher Delta (0.40 - 0.50)**: Selling options with higher Delta values involves choosing strike prices closer to the current stock price. These options have a higher likelihood of being exercised, which might be suitable if you are willing to potentially sell your stock but want to capture more premium.

> *Example*: If MSFT's stock price is $320, and you sell a call option with a Delta of 0.60 with a $325 strike price, you are choosing a strike price only 5 points above the current price. The higher Delta suggests a greater likelihood that MSFT will reach or exceed $325, leading to a higher premium but also a greater chance of having to sell your shares.

- **DTE (Days to Expiration)**: Days to Expiration (DTE) refers to the number of days remaining until the option contract expires. The expiration date is a critical component of the covered call strategy, as it affects the premium you receive, the likelihood of the option being exercised, and the management of the trade.
    - **Short-Term Options**: Options with shorter DTE (e.g., 1 to 2 weeks) typically offer lower premiums but provide more frequent opportunities for income. They also require more active management as the expiration date approaches.
    Example: Selling a call option on MSFT with a 2-week expiration period might offer a premium of $2 per share. While this provides a quick income opportunity, it also means you will need to reassess your position more frequently.
    - **Long-Term Options**: Options with longer DTE (e.g., 1 to 3 months) offer higher premiums due to the extended time value. However, they provide fewer opportunities for income and require less frequent management.
    Example: Selling a call option on MSFT with a 1-month expiration period might offer a premium of $4 per share. This higher premium compensates for the longer waiting period and reduces the need for frequent adjustments.

Example: If you own MSFT and anticipate a stable stock price, you might select a call option with a Delta of 0.30 and a 1-month expiration date. This setup allows you to earn a steady premium while retaining the potential for stock appreciation.

Case Study: MSFT Covered Call

Scenario: You own 100 shares of MSFT, currently trading at $320. You want to sell a covered call to generate income and are considering options with varying DTE and Delta values.

- **Select a Strike Price**: Decide on a strike price based on your outlook. For a stable outlook, choose a strike price above $320 with a lower Delta (e.g., $330 with Delta 0.30). For a more aggressive outlook, choose a closer strike price with a higher Delta (e.g., $325 with Delta 0.40).
- **Choose an Expiration Date**: Determine the expiration date based on your income goals and market outlook. Opt for a 1-month expiration date to balance premium income and management effort.
- **Execute the Trade**: Sell the chosen call option contract, e.g., a $330 strike price call option expiring in 1 month. Monitor the stock price and option Delta regularly to manage your position.

Example Trade Execution:

- **Stock Price:** $320
- **Strike Price:** $330 (Delta 0.30)
- **Expiration Date:** 1 month
- **Premium Received:** $5 per share

By selling this call option, you receive $500 in premium income (100 shares × $5) while setting a strike price that provides a good balance between premium income and the likelihood of having to sell your shares.

5.2.3 Execute the Trade

To execute a covered call:

- **Sell the Call Option**: Enter an order to sell the call option with your chosen strike price and expiration date. You will receive the premium for this option.

- **Hold the Stock**: Continue to hold the stock position. Your obligation is to deliver the stock if the option is exercised.

Example: sell a call option with a $170 strike price for Johnson & Johnson, expiring in one month, and receive a premium of $3 per share.

After executing the trade, monitoring and managing your covered call position is crucial:

- **Track Stock Price Movement**: Keep an eye on the stock price relative to the strike price. If the stock price approaches or exceeds the strike price, be prepared for the possibility of the option being exercised.

- **Adjust as Needed**: If market conditions change or your outlook shifts, you may need to adjust your position. This can include rolling the option to a different strike price or expiration date.

Example: if JNJ's stock price rises significantly, consider rolling the call option to a higher strike price or a later expiration date to capture more premium and maintain your position.

5.3 Managing Covered Calls

Once you have executed a covered call, the management and adjustment of the trade are essential to maximizing profit and managing risk. This section explores strategies and techniques for effectively managing and adjusting your covered call positions. We will cover key concepts such as monitoring your positions, making adjustments based on market conditions, and optimizing your outcomes.

Effective management begins with diligent monitoring of your covered call position. Regularly review the following aspects:

- **Stock Price Movement**: Keep an eye on the underlying stock's price relative to the strike price of your call option. If the stock price approaches or exceeds the strike price, it may increase the likelihood of the option being exercised.
  Example: If you sold a covered call with a $330 strike price on Microsoft Corporation (MSFT), and MSFT's price rises to $328, you need to be prepared for potential exercise if the stock continues to climb.

- **Option Premium**: Track the premium received from selling the call option. The premium's value can change as the stock price, time to expiration, and volatility fluctuate.
  Example: If the premium for your covered call decreases significantly, it might indicate a decrease in the option's time value or implied volatility, which could affect your decision-making.

- **Days to Expiration (DTE)**: Monitor the DTE as it decreases. Options lose value more quickly as they approach expiration (time decay). This is a key factor in managing your position and deciding when to take action.
  Example: With 10 days remaining until expiration, you might observe accelerated time decay. This could influence your decision to close, roll, or adjust the position.

- **Implied Volatility (IV)**: Implied volatility affects the option's premium. Higher IV generally increases premiums, while lower IV reduces them. Keeping track of IV can help you make better decisions about managing your covered call.

5.4 Adjusting Covered Calls

Adjusting a covered call becomes necessary when the trade's risk/reward dynamics shift, either because the underlying stock moves sharply or time passes without the expected outcome. Adjustments can help:

- **Avoid Assignment**: If the stock price is approaching the call's strike price, you might adjust to avoid being assigned.

- **Capture More Premium**: As market conditions change, you may want to generate additional income.

- **Mitigate Losses**: If the trade is moving against you, adjustments can help reduce potential losses.

- **Improve Overall Return**: Adjustments can turn a marginally profitable trade into a more lucrative one.

5.4.1 Rolling the Covered Call

Rolling involves closing the existing covered call position and opening a new one with different terms. This strategy is useful if you want to extend the trade, adjust the strike price, or capture additional premium.

- **Rolling Up**: If the stock price rises significantly, you might roll up the covered call to a higher strike price to avoid having your stock called

away and to increase the profit potential (stock price appreciation). There is a net cost for rolling up.
Example: If MSFT's stock rises to $340, and your original covered call has a $330 strike price, you can roll up by buying back the $330 call and selling a new call with a $340 strike price, extending the expiration if desired.

- **Rolling Down**: If the stock price falls and you want to adjust the strike price to a lower level while capturing some additional premium, rolling down can be beneficial.
Example: If MSFT's stock falls to $310 and you have a $330 call, you might roll down to a $320 strike price to collect some premium while adjusting for the lower stock price.

- **Rolling Out**: Extending the expiration date of your covered call can provide additional time for the stock to rise and increase the premium you can collect.
Example: If your covered call is set to expire in a week, and you want to extend it for another month, you can roll out by closing the current position and opening a new call option with a longer expiration date.

- **Rolling Up and Out**: This combination is useful when the stock price rises above the strike price, and you want to both avoid assignment and potentially capture more premium. Buy back the current call option and sell a new call with a higher strike price and a later expiration date.
Example: You sold a $50 call, and the stock has risen to $53. Instead of letting the stock get called away, you buy back the $50 call and sell a $55 call with an expiration date two months later. This move allows you to benefit from further upside in the stock while generating additional income from the new call option.

Adjustments may be necessary based on significant stock price movements. Here are some strategies:

- **If the Stock Rises**: If the stock price rises substantially, you may need to roll up the position to avoid having your stock called away or to capture additional premium.
Example: If MSFT's stock price surges to $350, and you have a covered call with a $330 strike price, rolling up to a higher strike price or closing the position might be advisable.

- **If the Stock Falls**: If the stock price falls significantly, consider rolling down to a lower strike price to continue collecting premium while adjusting for the new stock price.
  Example: If MSFT's stock price drops to $300, rolling down the strike price from $330 to $310 can help you manage the position and continue earning income.

5.4.2 Converting the Position into a Collar

Collars will be discussed deeply in the upcoming volume of the series: *The Option Trader's Income Blueprint: Unleash the Power of Advanced Income Strategies*. They can be considered adjustments of a covered call to be used If you are concerned about a potential decline in the underlying stock and want to protect your position.

You should purchase a put option at a strike price below the current stock price while maintaining your covered call position.

The put acts as insurance, limiting your potential loss if the stock price falls below the put's strike price.

This adjustment turns the covered call into a collar strategy, where your maximum profit and loss are capped.

Example: Suppose you sold a $50 call on a stock currently trading at $48. To protect against a drop in the stock price, you buy a $45 put. Now, if the stock falls below $45, your losses are limited, while you still have the potential to profit if the stock rises to $50.

5.4.3 Closing the Covered Call

Closing the covered call involves buying back the call option before expiration. This is often done if you wish to avoid having the stock called away or if you believe it's better to re-enter the position under more favorable conditions.

- **When to Close**: Consider closing the position if the stock price has approached or exceeded the strike price, or if there is a significant change in your outlook or strategy.
  Example: If MSFT's stock price rises to $335 and you are concerned about the possibility of your shares being called away, you might buy back the $330 call option to close the position and prevent the exercise of the option.

- **Cost of Closing**: When closing, you may incur a loss if the current option premium is higher than what you initially received. Evaluate whether the cost of closing justifies the benefit of avoiding a potential sale of the stock.

Example: If you received $4 for the covered call and it is now trading at $6 due to the stock price increase, you would incur a $2 per share loss to close the position.

5.4.4 Case Study: Managing a Covered Call on MSFT

Case Study: Managing a Covered Call on MSFT

Scenario: You sold a covered call on MSFT with a strike price of $330, an expiration date of 1 month, and received a $5 premium.

- **Day 10**: MSFT's stock price is at $325. The option premium is still relatively high. You decide to **roll up** by buying back the $330 call and selling a new call with a $340 strike price, extending the expiration by 2 weeks. This allows you to potentially capture more premium if the stock continues to rise.
- **Day 20**: MSFT's stock price has risen to $335. The option premium has decreased. The Delta of the call option is now closer to 0.60. You decide to close the position by buying back the $340 call for a higher price than you initially received. You evaluate the situation and choose to re-enter with a new covered call with a higher strike price or a different expiration date.

5.4.5 Case Study: Covered Call Strategy in Action

Case Study: Covered Call Strategy on MSFT

Company: Microsoft Corporation (MSFT)

- **Current Stock Price**: $320
- **Dividend Yield**: 0.9%
- **Premium Received**: $5 per share
- **Strike Price**: $330
- **Expiration Date**: 1 month

Implementation

- **Stock Purchase**: Purchase 100 shares of MSFT at $320 per share, requiring $32,000.
- **Sell Call Option**: Sell a call option with a $330 strike price and receive a premium of $5 per share, totaling $500.
- **Manage Position**: Monitor MSFT's stock price relative to the strike price. If MSFT's price remains below $330, you keep the $500 premium and can sell another call option in the next cycle. If MSFT's price exceeds $330, you may need to sell your shares at $330, realizing a capital gain plus the premium received.

Performance Analysis

- **Stock Price Below $330**: The option expires worthless, and you keep the $500 premium and any dividends received.
- **Stock Price Above $330**: The option is exercised, and you sell your shares at $330, realizing a gain of $10 per share ($330 - $320), plus the $5 premium, totaling a $1,500 profit ($1,000 from capital gain + $500 from premium).

5.5 Estimating Capital Requirements

Understanding the capital required to implement a covered call strategy is important for effective planning and risk management. Here's a breakdown of how to estimate the necessary capital:

- **Stock Purchase**: to execute a covered call, you must own or purchase the underlying stock. The capital required is the price of the stock multiplied by the number of shares you intend to use in the strategy.
  Example: If JNJ is trading at $165 and you wish to sell one call option contract, which represents 100 shares, you need $16,500 (100 shares × $165) to purchase the stock.

- **Premium Received**: the premium received from selling the call option reduces the effective capital requirement. This premium is yours to keep, regardless of whether the option is exercised.
  Example: If you receive $3 per share in premium, for 100 shares, you will earn $300 (100 shares × $3), which reduces the effective capital requirement to $16,200 ($16,500 - $300).

- **Managing Multiple Positions**: if you plan to implement covered calls on multiple stocks or multiple contracts, you need to account for the total capital required to purchase the stocks and the premiums received from each position.
Example: If you hold covered calls on three different stocks, each with 100 shares and premiums of $3, $2.50, and $3.50 respectively, you will need to aggregate the capital requirements for each stock while factoring in the total premiums received

5.6 CONCLUSION

The covered call strategy is a powerful tool for generating income from stocks you already own. By selecting the right stocks, choosing appropriate strike prices and expiration dates, and managing your positions effectively, you can enhance your investment income and reduce risks. With careful planning and execution, covered calls can become a cornerstone of your option trading strategy, providing a steady stream of income and contributing to your overall investment success.

In the following sections, we will explore additional strategies and advanced techniques to further enhance your option trading expertise.

CHAPTER 6

CASH-SECURED PUTS – EARNING WHILE YOU WAIT

Imagine you're an investor with a strong belief in a particular stock's long-term potential, but you're hesitant to buy it at its current price. What if there was a way to potentially acquire that stock at a lower price while earning income in the meantime? This is where the cash-secured put strategy comes into play. This chapter delves into the cash-secured put strategy, providing a comprehensive understanding of how it works, its benefits, risks, and practical applications. We will explore detailed examples, step-by-step guides, and strategies for managing and optimizing this approach.

The primary purpose of this chapter is to equip investors with a thorough understanding of the cash-secured put strategy, a powerful tool for generating income while waiting for a favorable buying opportunity. We aim to elucidate the mechanics of this strategy, demonstrate its practical applications with real-life examples, and provide actionable insights into selecting the right stocks and managing the positions effectively. By the end of this chapter, readers should have a solid grasp of how to implement cash-secured puts to enhance their income generation and improve their investment approach.

6.1 THE PURPOSE OF CASH SECURED PUTS

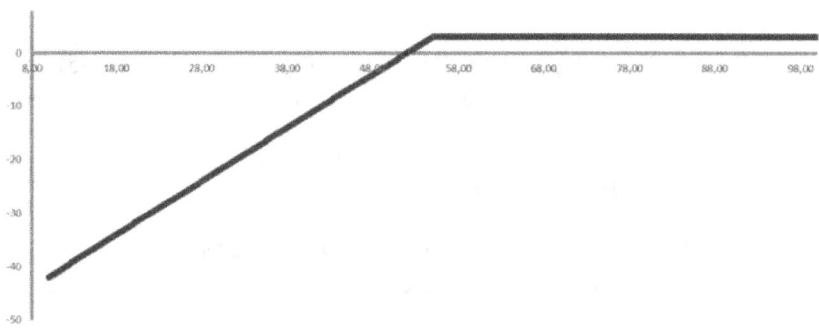

Figure 21 - Cash-Secured Put Payoff

A cash-secured put involves selling a put option while holding enough cash to buy the underlying stock if the option is exercised. In essence, you're agreeing to buy the stock at a specific price (strike price) if the stock falls below that price by the option's expiration date. In return for this commitment, you receive a premium from selling the put option.

- **Income Generation:** The primary objective of a cash-secured put is to generate income by selling a put option. The premium received from the sale is yours to keep, regardless of whether the option is exercised. This premium can serve as a consistent source of income, much like the dividends or interest payments in other investment strategies.

- **Potential to Buy Stocks at a Discount:** One of the unique advantages of a cash-secured put is the opportunity to purchase a stock at a lower price. If the stock price drops below the strike price and the put option is exercised, you effectively buy the stock at a price below the current market value, minus the premium received. This can be a strategic way to acquire stocks you believe in at a discount.

- **Enhancing Returns**: For investors who are bullish on a stock but prefer to wait for a more attractive entry point, the cash-secured put offers a way to enhance returns. Even if the stock remains above the strike price and the put is not exercised, you still retain the premium, which adds to your overall return. This approach allows you to benefit from stable or slowly rising stock prices while generating additional income from the option premium.

A cash-secured put includes the following components:

- **Put Option**: A financial contract that gives the buyer the right to sell the underlying stock at the strike price before the option expires.

- **Strike Price**: The price at which you agree to buy the stock if the put option is exercised.

- **Premium**: The income you receive for selling the put option, which is yours to keep regardless of whether the option is exercised or not.

- **Cash Reserve**: The amount of cash set aside to purchase the stock if required.

6.2 Step by Step Guide to Executing a Cash Secured Put

Here's a step-by-step breakdown of how a cash-secured put works:

- **Sell a Put Option**: Choose a stock you are willing to own and sell a put option with a specific strike price and expiration date.

- **Receive Premium**: Upon selling the put option, you receive a premium which provides immediate income.

- **Hold Cash**: Maintain sufficient cash in your brokerage account to cover the cost of buying the stock at the strike price if the option is exercised.

- **Wait for Expiration**: If the stock price remains above the strike price, the option expires worthless, and you keep the premium as profit.

- **Stock Purchase (if exercised)**: If the stock price falls below the strike price, the option may be exercised, and you will need to buy the stock at the strike price. However, you keep the premium received from selling the put.

Example: Suppose you are interested in buying shares of Company XYZ, which is currently trading at $50. You decide to sell a cash-secured put option with a strike price of $45, expiring in one month, and receive a $2 premium per share. You reserve $4,500 in cash (for 100 shares) to cover the potential purchase.

- **Scenario 1**: If XYZ's stock price remains above $45, the put option expires worthless, and you keep the $200 premium as profit.

- **Scenario 2**: If XYZ's stock price falls to $40, the option may be exercised, and you purchase 100 shares at $45 each, costing $4,500. You still keep the $200 premium, effectively reducing your net purchase price to $43 per share.

6.2.1 Choosing the Right Underlying Asset

When selecting stocks for cash-secured puts, consider the following criteria:

- **Stock Quality**: Choose high-quality, fundamentally strong stocks with good growth prospects or solid dividends. Stocks with stable or predictable performance reduce the risk of significant price drops, which could affect the attractiveness of the put option strategy.

- **Volatility**: Higher volatility can lead to higher premiums, but it also increases the risk of the stock price falling below the strike price.

- **Liquidity**: Ensure the stock has sufficient trading volume and options liquidity to enter and exit positions easily.

- **Strike Price and Expiration**: Select a strike price and expiration date that align with your investment goals and risk tolerance.

- **Attractive Entry Price**: The stock should be one you are willing to own at a lower price. This means selecting stocks that are fundamentally strong and trading below their intrinsic value or at a discount.

For example, if you are considering a cash-secured put on Apple Inc. (AAPL), you might look for factors such as its robust financials, strong market position, and historical performance. You might also analyze its volatility and ensure that there are liquid options available.

Case Study: MSFT Cash-Secured Put

Company: Microsoft Corporation (MSFT)

- **Current Stock Price**: $320
- **Dividend Yield**: 0.9%
- **Trading Volume**: High

Strategy:

- **Sell Put Option**: Choose a put option with a strike price of $310 and an expiration date one month away.

Premium Received: $5 per share

Why MSFT?

- **Desirable Entry Point**: Microsoft is a fundamentally strong company. Selling puts allows you to potentially buy MSFT at a price lower than the current market value, aligning with your investment goals.
- **Liquidity**: Microsoft options are highly liquid, facilitating smooth execution and management of the put strategy.
- **Stable Performance**: Microsoft's strong financials and market position contribute to its stability, reducing the risk of significant price drops.

Potential Outcomes:

- **Stock Price Above $310**: The option expires worthless, and you keep the $5 premium per share.
- **Stock Price Below $310**: You may be required to purchase the stock at $310. With the $5 premium received, your effective purchase price is $305 per share.

6.2.2 Setting Up the Trade

Once you have selected the stock, the next step is to choose the strike price and expiration date for the call option:

- **Strike Price**: The strike price should be lower than the current stock price. This is because you are agreeing to buy the stock at that price if the option is exercised. By selecting a strike price below the current stock price, you increase the chances that the option will expire without being exercised, allowing you to keep the premium. However, if the stock does fall to or below this price, you will be purchasing the stock at a discount compared to its previous price.

- **Expiration Date**: The expiration date should align with your market outlook and objectives. Shorter expiration periods (e.g., weekly or monthly options) allow you to generate income more frequently but usually offer lower premiums. Conversely, longer expiration periods offer higher premiums but reduce the frequency of income opportunities and may expose you to market risks for an extended period.

In the cash-secured put strategy, the trade setup is essential to balance the risk and reward. As described in the Covered Call chapter, two key factors in setting up your strategy are **Delta** and **Days to Expiration (DTE)**. Understanding these factors will help you make informed decisions about selecting the right strike prices and expiration dates for your options:

- **Determine Your Income Goals**: Decide how much income you wish to generate and how frequently. Selling puts with shorter DTE (Days to Expiration) will allow you to collect premiums more often, which can be beneficial if you want regular income and are comfortable managing multiple trades. On the other hand, selling puts with longer DTE can yield higher premiums but requires a longer commitment and less frequent income collection.

- **Assess Market Conditions**: Analyze the stock's price movements and volatility. If you expect the stock to remain stable or gradually decline, you might choose a lower Delta and longer DTE. A lower Delta indicates a lower probability of the option being in the money at expiration, which could increase the chances of the option expiring worthless. If you anticipate significant price movements, consider a higher Delta and shorter DTE options, which provide more immediate income but increase the likelihood of acquiring the stock.

- **Select Appropriate Strike Price and Expiration Date**: Based on your market analysis and income goals, choose a strike price that aligns with your outlook. Match this with an expiration date that fits your desired income frequency and risk tolerance. The right combination will depend on your specific objectives, whether you prioritize regular income, minimizing the risk of stock acquisition, or seeking potential stock ownership at a favorable price.

Here below a detailed description about the rules you might follow to choose delta and DTE for a cash-secured put option strategy:

- **Delta:** As described in the previous chapters, delta measures the sensitivity of an option's price to changes in the price of the underlying asset. For put options, delta is a negative value, typically ranging from -1 to 0. Here's a quick reminder of its meaning:
    - **Delta Value**: A delta of -0.40 means that for every $1 decrease in the stock price, the price of the put option will increase by $0.40, and vice versa.
    - **Probabilities**: Delta can also be interpreted as the approximate probability that the option will be in-the-money at expiration. For instance, a delta of -0.30 suggests a 30% chance that the option will end up in-the-money.

  When setting up a cash-secured put trade, you should choose a delta that reflects your risk tolerance and market outlook. A higher delta (e.g., -0.40) indicates a higher probability of the option being exercised, thus potentially leading to the purchase of the stock at the strike price. Conversely, a lower delta (e.g., -0.20) suggests a lower likelihood of exercise and generally lower risk.

  Example: Suppose you are considering selling a put option on XYZ Corporation, which is currently trading at $100. You look at two potential strike prices:
    - **Strike Price A**: $95, with a delta of -0.40. The -0.40 delta indicates a 40% chance that the option will be exercised. This option is more sensitive to price changes and might be riskier.
    - **Strike Price B**: $90, with a delta of -0.20. The -0.20 delta indicates a 20% chance that the option will be exercised. This option is less sensitive to price changes and presents a lower risk but lower premium.

- **DTE (Days to Expiration):** Time decay (theta) affects the value of options as expiration approaches, and understanding this is crucial for managing cash-secured puts.

  As an option approaches its expiration date, its time value decreases, which generally benefits the seller. For put options, this

means that as time passes, the value of the option decreases if the stock price remains above the strike price.

When setting up a cash-secured put trade, choose an expiration date that matches your strategy. Shorter DTE options (e.g., 10 days) provide quicker time decay benefits and might be suitable for tactical trades. Longer DTE options (e.g., 30 days) offer higher premiums and may suit strategic trades where you're willing to wait for potential price movements.

Example: Imagine you're evaluating two put options on ABC Inc., which is currently trading at $75:

- **Option A**: Strike price of $70, expiring in 30 days, with a premium of $3. With 30 days until expiration, the premium is higher due to greater time value. This option provides more time for the stock price to fluctuate, leading to higher premiums but potentially higher risk.
- **Option B**: Strike price of $70, expiring in 10 days, with a premium of $1.50. With only 10 days until expiration, the premium is lower as time decay has reduced its value. The risk is reduced because there's less time for significant price movements.

Case Study: Cash Secured Put on ORCL

You are considering selling cash-secured puts on ORCL, which is trading at $120:

- **Option 1**: Strike price of $115, delta of -0.45, DTE of 45 days.
- **Option 2**: Strike price of $115, delta of -0.25, DTE of 15 days.

Trade Setup:

- **Option 1**: The longer DTE provide a more conservative approach with potentially higher premiums. This may be suitable if you want to collect more premium. The trader can evaluate to choose a lower delta to reduce the probability of getting assigned (therefore the premium will be lower)
- **Option 2**: The shorter DTE offer a more aggressive approach, with quicker time decay benefits and a higher likelihood of the option being

exercised. This might suit a more tactical approach if you want to manage positions more frequently.

6.2.3 Execute the Trade

To execute a cash-secured put:

- **Sell the Put Option**: Enter an order to sell the put option with your chosen strike price and expiration date. You will receive the premium for this option.

- **Hold the Cash Reserve**: Keep enough cash in your brokerage account to cover the cost of buying the stock at the strike price if the option is exercised.

After executing the trade, monitoring and managing your cash-secured put position is crucial:

- **Tracking Stock Price**: Regularly monitor the stock price and market conditions. Significant price movements might require adjustments to your strategy.

- **Adjust as Needed**: If market conditions change or your outlook shifts, you may need to adjust your position. This can include rolling the option to a different strike price or expiration date.

Example: If Company ABC's stock drops to $60 and you want to avoid purchasing the stock, you might roll the put by buying back the $65 strike put option and selling a new put option with a $60 strike price and a later expiration. This allows you to collect additional premium while adjusting for the new market conditions.

Case Study: Cash Secured Put on TSLA

Background: In a volatile market, you are interested in acquiring shares of Tesla Inc. (TSLA), which is currently trading at $600. You decide to use the cash-secured put strategy to potentially buy TSLA at a lower price while generating income.

Implementation:

- **Sell Put Option**: You sell a put option with a strike price of $550, expiring in one month, and receive a premium of $15 per share.
- **Reserve Cash**: You reserve $55,000 (for 100 shares) to cover the potential purchase of TSLA if the option is exercised.

Outcomes:

- **Stock Price Above $550**: If TSLA's stock price remains above $550, the put option expires worthless. You keep the $1,500 premium as profit.
- **Stock Price Below $550**: If TSLA's stock price falls to $500, the option is exercised, and you buy 100 shares at $550 each, costing $55,000. The premium received lowers your effective purchase price to $535 per share ($550 strike price - $15 premium).

6.3 Managing Cash-Secured Puts

Cash-secured puts are a popular strategy among options traders looking to generate income while potentially acquiring stocks at a desired price. However, like all trading strategies, they carry risks. When a cash-secured put trade goes against you, it can create a challenging situation. This section explores in detail how to adjust cash-secured puts when the trade moves unfavorably, providing actionable strategies and real-life examples to guide you through the process.

When you sell a cash-secured put, you agree to buy the underlying stock at the strike price if the option is exercised. If the stock price falls below the strike price, you might face the obligation to buy the stock at a higher price than its current market value. This situation can lead to potential losses or require adjustments to avoid an undesirable outcome.

When engaging in a cash-secured put strategy, staying vigilant about key factors such as the stock price movement, option premium, days to expiration (DTE), and implied volatility (IV) is crucial. Understanding and monitoring these elements can help you manage your position effectively and make informed decisions. Here's how to approach each of these aspects:

- **Stock Price Movement**: One of the most critical factors to monitor is the underlying stock's price relative to the strike price of the put option you sold. If the stock price drops toward or below the strike price, the likelihood of the option being exercised increases.

Example: Suppose you sold a cash-secured put on Apple Inc. (AAPL) with a strike price of $150. If AAPL's price declines to $152, you need to be aware that further declines could lead to the option being exercised, requiring you to purchase the stock at $150.

- **Option Premium**: The premium received from selling the put option is a crucial component of your income. However, the value of this premium can fluctuate based on the underlying stock's price, time to expiration, and changes in implied volatility.

  Example If you initially received a $3.00 premium for selling a put option on stock with a $600 strike price, you might observe that the premium decreases as the stock price stabilizes above $600. This decrease might reflect reduced implied volatility or the passage of time.

- **Days to Expiration (DTE)**: As the option approaches its expiration date, the time value of the option erodes, a phenomenon known as time decay. Monitoring the DTE helps you understand how quickly the option is losing value and informs your decision on whether to adjust or close the position.

  Example: Imagine you have sold a cash-secured put on Amazon.com, Inc. (AMZN) with 30 days to expiration. As time passes and the DTE decreases to 10 days, you'll notice an acceleration in time decay, particularly if AMZN's stock price remains stable above the strike price.

- **Implied Volatility (IV)**: Implied volatility reflects market expectations of future volatility and has a direct impact on the option's premium. Higher IV typically results in higher option premiums, while lower IV leads to lower premiums.

  Example: If you sold a cash-secured put on Netflix, Inc. (NFLX) when implied volatility was high, you might have received a premium of $5.00. If IV subsequently drops, the option's premium might decrease to $3.00, even if the stock price remains relatively unchanged.

6.4 Adjusting Cash Secured Puts

6.4.1 Rolling the Put Option

Rolling involves closing the existing put position and opening a new one with different parameters, such as a different strike price (roll down) or expiration date (roll out) or both (roll out and down). The strategy is the same explained in the covered call chapter.

Rolling can help manage risk, extend the duration of the trade, and potentially improve the position's profitability:

- **Rolling Up**: Rolling up is useful when the stock price increases, and you want to increase the strike price to collect a higher premium or take advantage of the stock's upward momentum. Buy back the original put option and sell a new put at a higher strike price.
  Example: You sold a $45 put, and the stock has risen to $50. You could buy back the $45 put and sell a $48 or $50 put to increase the premium collected or position yourself closer to the current stock price.

- **Rolling Down**: Rolling down without extending the expiration is appropriate when you want to reduce the strike price without increasing the trade duration. Buy back the original put option and sell a new put at a lower strike price, but with the same expiration date. This can lead to net costs.
  Example: If you sold a $50 put, and the stock is now at $47, you could buy back the $50 put and sell a $48 put with the same expiration. This lowers the strike price and reduces the potential loss if the stock declines further.

- **Rolling Out**: Extending the expiration date of your cash-secured put can provide additional time for the stock to rise and increase the premium you can collect.
  Example: If your cash-secured is set to expire in a week, and you want to extend it for another month, you can roll out by closing the current position and opening a new cash-secure put with a longer expiration date.

- **Rolling Down and Out**: Rolling down and out is suitable when the stock price has declined, and you want to reduce the strike price to avoid immediate assignment, while extending the duration of the trade to give the stock time to recover. Buy back the original put option and sell a new put with a lower strike price, at the same time extend the expiration date by selling the new put with a later expiration.

Example: Suppose you sold a $50 put, and the stock has dropped to $45. To avoid assignment, you buy back the $50 put and sell a new $45 put with an expiration date further out. This reduces your strike price and extends the trade's timeline.

6.4.2. Converting the Position into a Credit Spread

This adjustment is useful when you want to cap your risk and reduce potential losses by converting the cash-secured put into a credit spread (detailed in the subsequent of the series: *The Option Trader's Income Blueprint: Unleash the Power of Advanced Income Strategies*).

To convert a cash-secured put into a credit spread, you should buy a further out-of-the-money put to cap the downside risk.

Example: If you sold a $50 put, and the stock is now at $48, you could buy a $45 put. Potentially you can also replace the original put with a new $47 put (i.e. buy back the $50 put and sell the $47 one), creating a $47/$45 credit spread. This adjustment limits your maximum loss to the difference between the strike prices, minus the premium received.

6.4.3 Converting the Position into a Strangle / Straddle

Converting a cash-secured put into a strangle or straddle (clearly detailed in the subsequent volume of the series: *The Option Trader's Income Blueprint: Unleash the Power of Advanced Income Strategies*) is an advanced adjustment strategy that can help traders manage risk, increase income potential, and capitalize on market conditions. These strategies involve adding additional options positions to the existing put, creating a multi-legged strategy that benefits from specific market movements.

- **Converting a Cash-Secured Put into a Strangle:** This adjustment can be used when the stock price goes against your cash-secured position. The aim of the strategy is to enhance the overall premium income to increase the buffer against unexpected market movements.
  A strangle involves selling a call option at a higher strike price while keeping your existing short put position. The call option is typically

out of the money, meaning its strike price is above the current stock price.

Example: Suppose you have sold a cash-secured put on XYZ stock at a strike price of $50, and the stock is trading around $48. You could sell an out-of-the-money call option, say at a $55 strike price.

- If the stock price stays between $50 and $55 at expiration, both the put and call options expire worthless, and you keep the premium from both.
- If the stock price falls below $50, you might be assigned the stock at $50, but you still keep the premium from both the put and call options, reducing your effective purchase price. If you want to reduce the possibility of being assigned, you can close the position before expiration.
- If the stock price rises above $55, the call option could be exercised, and you might have to sell (short) the stock at $55. You still keep the premium from both the put and the call option, which help reduce the loss. If you want to reduce the possibility of being assigned, you can close the position before expiration.

- **Converting a Cash-Secured Put into a Straddle:** Converting a cash-secure put into a straddle (detailed in the next volume of the series: *The Option Trader's Income Blueprint: Unleash the Power of Advanced Income Strategies*) it's a more aggressive strategy compared to a strangle, as it involves selling a call and a put at the same strike price.

To convert a cash-secured put into a straddle, you would sell an at-the-money call option at the same strike price as the put option you have already sold.

Example: Continuing with the XYZ stock example, if you sold a $50 put option, and the stock is trading at $50, you could sell a $50 call option, creating a straddle.

- If the stock price remains close to $50 at expiration, both options expire worthless, and you keep the premium from both.
- If the stock price drops significantly below $50, you might be assigned the stock at $50, and you could face a loss if the stock continues to fall. If you want to reduce the possibility of being assigned, you can close the position before expiration.

- If the stock price rises significantly above $50, you might be forced to sell (short) the stock at $50 if the call is exercised. You still keep the premium from both the put and the call option, which help reduce the loss. If you want to reduce the possibility of being assigned, you can close the position before expiration.

6.4.4 Closing the Cash-Secured Put

Exiting the position early involves closing the put option before expiration, even if it results in a loss.

The strategy can be useful to cut losses and avoid further risk if the stock price continues to move unfavorably.

- **Analyze the Position**: Determine if the potential losses from continuing the position outweigh the benefits of holding.

- **Calculate the Cost**: Assess the cost of buying back the put option and compare it to the potential losses if the position is maintained.

- **Execute the Exit**: Buy back the put option and close the position to limit further losses.

Example:

- **Initial Position**: You sold a cash-secured put with a $60 strike price, and the stock has dropped to $50 with a significant decline in premium value.

- **Exit Action**: If the cost to buy back the put option is reasonable compared to potential further declines, closing the position early might be prudent to avoid additional losses.

6.4.5 Real-Life Examples of Adjusting Cash-Secured Puts

Example 1: Rolling to a New Strike Price and Expiration

- **Initial Position**: You sold a cash-secured put with a $75 strike price, and the stock has fallen to $70.
- **Rolling Action**: To manage the risk, you buy back the $75 put and sell a new put option with a $70 strike price and an expiration date 45 days out. This adjustment aligns the strike price with the current stock price and extends the duration of the trade. This adjustment can lead to a net cost.

Example 2: Adding Protective Positions

- **Initial Position**: You sold a cash-secured put with a $55 strike price, and the stock is trading at $50.
- **Protection Action**: To hedge against further declines, you buy a put option with a $45 strike price. This additional put will protect you from substantial losses if the stock continues to drop.

Example 3: Exiting the Position Early

- **Initial Position**: You sold a cash-secured put with a $40 strike price, and the stock has fallen to $35. With only a few days left until expiration and a significant drop in stock price, you decide to exit early.
- **Exit Action**: You buy back the $40 put option at a loss, avoiding potential further declines and locking in the loss at a manageable level.

6.5 Estimating Capital Requirements for Cash-Secured Puts

When engaging in a cash-secured put strategy, estimating the capital requirements is crucial for effective planning and risk management. This strategy involves selling put options while holding enough cash to buy the underlying stock if the option is exercised. This section will provide a comprehensive breakdown of how to estimate the capital requirements for implementing and maintaining a cash-secured put position.

To effectively manage a cash-secured put, you need to estimate both the required cash reserve and any potential additional capital needs.

- **Cash Reserve**: this is the amount of cash needed in case the option expires in the money and it is computed as Strike Price × Number of Shares.
  Ensure that the cash reserve is kept liquid and accessible, as it may be required to fulfill the purchase obligation if the option is exercised.
  The cash reserve should be held in a cash or cash-equivalent account to ensure availability when needed.
  Example:
    - **Stock**: XYZ Corporation
    - **Strike Price**: $50
    - **Number of Shares**: 100
    - **Required Cash Reserve** = $50×100=$5,000

  In this example, you would need to set aside $5,000 to cover the potential purchase of 100 shares of XYZ at $50 per share if the put option is exercised.

- **Total Capital**: this is the total amount of cash a trader needs to set aside to implement the cash-secured strategy. The premium collected (short put) will reduce the overall capital need (Required Cash Reserve−Premium Received).
  The premium received reduces the effective capital requirement but should not be relied upon as a buffer. Ensure sufficient cash reserve to cover the full strike price if the option is exercised.
  Example:
    - **Strike Price**: $50
    - **Number of Shares**: 100
    - **Premium Received**: $2 per share
    - **Premium Received** =$2×100=$200
    - **Total Capital Requirement** =$5,000−$200=$4,800

  In this scenario, the initial capital outlay, considering the premium income, would be $4,800. This amount reflects the net cash needed to implement the strategy after accounting for the premium received from selling the put option.

- **Managing Multiple Positions**: if you plan to implement cash-secured puts on multiple stocks or multiple contracts, you need to account for the total capital required to purchase the stocks and the premiums received from each position.
  Diversify positions to mitigate risk, but ensure that capital is available for each position's required reserve.

Example: If you hold cash-secured puts on two different stocks, each with 100 shares and premiums of $3, $2.50 and strikes $100.0, $80.00 respectively, you will need to aggregate the capital requirements for each stock (cash reserve) while factoring in the total premiums received.

Market conditions can affect the premium received and the stock's price volatility, influencing your capital requirements. Here's how to adjust:

- **Volatility Changes**: Higher volatility increases premium income, reducing the effective capital requirement. Conversely, lower volatility may decrease premiums, necessitating a higher cash reserve.

- **Stock Price Movements**: If the stock price moves significantly, adjust the cash reserve accordingly. For instance, if the stock price drops below the strike price, you might need to increase the reserve to cover potential purchase costs.

Regularly review and update your capital estimates based on the latest market conditions and premiums and always try to maintain a buffer of additional cash to handle unexpected changes or market volatility.

6.6 Conclusion

Cash-secured puts are a powerful strategy for generating steady income, especially in a market where you are confident about the underlying stock's long-term prospects. By selling puts, you receive premium income and potentially buy stocks you want to own at a lower price, combining income generation with value investing principles.

This strategy provides a dual benefit:

- **Income Generation**: the premiums collected from selling puts contribute to a steady income stream, enhancing your overall portfolio returns.
- **Stock Acquisition**: if the stock price drops below the strike price, you acquire shares at a price you're comfortable with, which can be a strategic entry point for long-term investment

CONCLUSION

HARNESSING THE POWER OF OPTION INCOME STRATEGIES

As we conclude our exploration of this volume, it's important to reflect on the most critical takeaways that will empower you on your journey to financial success. This eBook has equipped you with a thorough understanding of various strategies and techniques that can significantly enhance your trading endeavors. Here's a summary of the essential concepts and insights:

Key Takeaways

- **Foundational Knowledge**:
    - **Understanding Options Basics**: Fundamental concepts of options, including the different types (calls and puts) and their primary functions, to build a strong foundation for trading.
    - **Mastering the Greeks**: Deep understanding of the Greeks (Delta, Gamma, Theta, Vega) to analyze and predict options behavior, crucial for effective strategy implementation.
    - **Volatility and Its Impact**: The concept of volatility and its significant impact on options pricing, ensuring a comprehensive approach to your trading strategies.
    - **Asset Selection**: How to choose the most suitable assets, based on quantitative techniques aiming to assess the volatility, risk-

- **Income Generation**:
    - **Generating Income with Covered Calls**: Covered calls can earn regular premiums, providing a steady income stream while managing potential risks.
    - **Earning Consistent Returns with Cash-Secured Puts**: Cash-secured puts can turn market fluctuations into opportunities for consistent returns, offering a reliable method for income generation in options trading.

The Value of Income Strategies

The income strategies discussed in this first volume of *The Option Trader's Income Blueprint* provide practical and effective methods to enhance your financial outcomes. By applying these foundational strategies, such as covered calls and cash-secured puts, you can begin generating a steady stream of income and use your capital more efficiently. These strategies are designed to offer stability and growth, allowing you to capitalize on market movements and optimize your returns.

With the knowledge you've gained from this book, you are now equipped to take action. Start by applying the concepts and techniques to set up a basic option income portfolio. Focus on creating a clear plan, selecting appropriate strategies, and utilizing the tools you've learned about to enhance your trading performance.

Here are a few general steps to get started:

- **Start Small**: Begin with small trades and gradually increase your position size as you gain experience and confidence. Avoid putting too much capital at risk in the early stages.
- **Assess Your Portfolio**: Evaluate your current investments and identify opportunities to apply the covered call and cash-secured put strategies.
- **Choose Appropriate Strategies**: Select strategies that align with your market outlook and risk tolerance, focusing on the foundational techniques discussed in this volume.
- **Review and Adjust**: Regularly monitor your trades and portfolio, adjusting as necessary based on market conditions.
- **Commit to Continuous Learning**: While this book provides a strong foundation, remember that options trading is a complex field. Stay informed about market developments and consider exploring the

other volumes in this series to deepen your knowledge and refine your strategies.
- **Risk Management**: Prioritize risk management in every trade. Define your maximum acceptable loss and avoid chasing losses. Protecting your capital should always be your top priority.
- **Patience and Discipline**: Successful options trading requires patience and discipline. Stick to your trading plan, avoid impulsive decisions, and don't let emotions drive your trades.

This first volume is just the beginning of your journey in options trading. The knowledge and strategies you've learned here will serve as a crucial foundation, but to fully master options trading and unlock its full potential, it's important to continue your education by exploring the subsequent volumes in this series. Each volume builds on the last, offering more advanced strategies and insights that will help you achieve a comprehensive understanding of options trading.

So, take this important first step with confidence. Apply the insights you've gained, execute your strategies carefully, and watch as your financial objectives start to come within reach. The markets are full of opportunities, the journey continues with the next volume.

ANNEX

THE BLACK-SCHOLES AND BINOMIAL MODELS FOR OPTION PRICING

Option pricing is a cornerstone of modern finance, providing traders and investors with a framework for determining the fair value of options. Two of the most widely used models for this purpose are the Black-Scholes model and the Binomial model. This chapter will explore these models in detail, explaining how they work, their assumptions, and their practical applications in the world of options trading.

The Black-Scholes Model

The Black-Scholes model, introduced in 1973 by Fischer Black and Myron Scholes, revolutionized the field of financial economics by providing a mathematical formula for pricing European-style options. The model assumes that the price of the underlying asset follows a geometric Brownian motion with constant volatility and interest rates.

Key Assumptions of the Black-Scholes Model:

- **European Option**: The model applies to European options, which can only be exercised at expiration.

- **No Dividends**: The underlying asset does not pay dividends during the life of the option (though the model can be adjusted for dividends).

- **Constant Risk-Free Rate**: The risk-free interest rate is constant over the option's life.

- **Constant Volatility**: The volatility of the underlying asset's returns is constant.

- **Log-Normal Distribution**: The asset's returns are normally distributed (log-normal price distribution).

- **No Arbitrage**: There are no opportunities for arbitrage, meaning the price of the option reflects all available information.

The Black-Scholes formula for a European call option is given by:

$$C = S_0 N(d1) - Xe^{-rT} N(d2)$$

For a European put option:

$$P = Xe^{-rT} N(-d2) - S_0 N(-d1)$$

Where:

- C = Call option price
- P = Put option price
- S0 = Current price of the underlying asset
- X = Strike price of the option
- T = Time to expiration (in years)
- r = Risk-free interest rate
- N(d) = Cumulative distribution function of the standard normal distribution
- d1 and d2 are calculated as follows:

$$d1 = \frac{\ln\left(\frac{S_0}{X}\right) + \left(r + \frac{\sigma^2}{2}\right)T}{\sigma\sqrt{T}}$$

$$d2 = d1 - \sigma\sqrt{T}$$

- σ represents the volatility of the underlying asset
- N(d1) and N(d2) represent the probabilities that the option will end up in-the-money, adjusted for the time value of money.
- S₀N(d1) represents the present value of the expected payoff from owning the stock.

- $Xe^{-rT}N(d2)$ represents the present value of the expected cost of exercising the option.

Traders and analysts use the Black-Scholes model to estimate the fair value of European options. It is particularly useful for determining theoretical option prices and implied volatility. Implied volatility, extracted from the model by solving for σ, reflects the market's expectations of future volatility and is a crucial input for trading strategies.

Example: Pricing a European Call Option

Consider an option on a stock currently trading at $100, with a strike price of $105, 1 year until expiration, a risk-free rate of 5%, and a volatility of 20%.

- Plugging the values into the Black-Scholes formula:

$$d1 = \frac{\ln\left(\frac{100}{105}\right) + \left(0.05 + \frac{0.2^2}{2}\right)1}{0.2\sqrt{1}} = 0.106$$

$$d2 = 0.106 - 0.2 = -0.094$$

$$C = 100 N(0.106) - 105 e^{-0.05} N(-0.094)$$

- Using standard normal distribution tables or software to find N(d1) and N(d2):

$$C = 100 * 0.5424 - 105 * 0.9512 * 0.4624 = 6.80$$

So, the theoretical price of the call option is approximately $6.80.

The Binomial Model

The Binomial model, developed by Cox, Ross, and Rubinstein in 1979, is an alternative method for option pricing. Unlike the Black-Scholes model, which assumes continuous trading, the Binomial model works by breaking down the option's life into multiple discrete time intervals (steps). At each step, the price of the underlying asset can move up or down, creating a binomial tree of possible future prices.

Key Assumptions of the Binomial Model:

- **Discrete Time Intervals**: The option's life is divided into a finite number of intervals.

- **Two Possible Outcomes per Interval**: In each time step, the asset price can either move up by a factor u or down by a factor d.

- **No Arbitrage**: The model assumes no arbitrage opportunities.

- **European and American Options**: Unlike the Black-Scholes model, the Binomial model can price both European and American options (which can be exercised at any time before expiration).

Constructing the Binomial Tree:

- **Define the Time Steps**: The option's life is divided into n discrete intervals. For each interval, the price can move up or down.

- **Calculate the Up and Down Factors**:

$$u = e^{\sigma\sqrt{\Delta t}}$$

$$d = \frac{1}{u} = e^{-\sigma\sqrt{\Delta t}}$$

Where $\Delta t = \frac{T}{n}$ is the length of each time step.

- **Risk-Neutral Probability**: The probability of an upward move in a risk-neutral world is:

$$p = \frac{e^{r\Delta t} - d}{u - d}$$

- **Price the Option at Expiration**: At the final step (maturity), the option's value is the intrinsic value (max of 0 or St–X for calls, X–St for puts).

- **Work Backward**: Starting from the final step, work backward through the tree to determine the option's value at each preceding node using the formula:

$$C = e^{-r\Delta t} * (p * C_u + (1 - p) * C_d)$$

Where Cu and Cd are the option values at the up and down nodes, respectively.

The Binomial model is particularly useful for pricing American options, as it accounts for the possibility of early exercise. It also offers flexibility in handling varying conditions, such as changes in volatility or dividends.

Example: Pricing an American Call Option

Let's assume a stock is currently priced at $50, with a strike price of $52, volatility of 30%, risk-free rate of 5%, and time to expiration of 3 months (0.25 years). We'll divide the option's life into 3 steps.

- Calculate the Up and Down Factors:

$$\Delta t = \frac{0.25}{3} \approx 0.0833$$

$$u = e^{0.3\sqrt{0.0833}} = 1.0916$$

$$d = \frac{1}{u} = 0.9160$$

- Risk-Neutral Probability:

$$p = \frac{e^{0.05*0.0833} - 0.9160}{1.0916 - 0.9160} \approx 0.5373$$

- Construct the Binomial Tree: Start with the current stock price and calculate possible prices at each step.

- Price the Option: Start at the final nodes and work backward, applying the risk-neutral probability to calculate the option's value at each step.

Comparing the Black-Scholes and Binomial Models

- **Black-Scholes Model**:
    - **Advantages**:
        - **Analytical Simplicity**: The Black-Scholes model provides a straightforward, closed-form solution for pricing European options.
        - **Speed**: It is computationally less intensive than the Binomial model.

- **Widely Accepted**: It is the most widely recognized model in the finance industry, especially for pricing European-style options.
- **Limitations:**
  - Assumes constant volatility, which is often unrealistic.
  - Cannot accurately price American options or options with dividends without adjustments.

- Binomial Model:
  - **Advantages:**
    - **Flexibility**: The Binomial model can price American options and handle a wide range of conditions, such as varying volatility and dividends.
    - **Accuracy**: By increasing the number of steps, the Binomial model can closely approximate real market conditions, including early exercise.
    - **Modeling Complex Scenarios**: It is more adaptable to different types of exotic options and can be tailored to reflect specific market conditions.
  - **Limitations:**
    - **Computationally more intensive**, especially with a large number of steps.
    - **Requires more data input and detailed calculation**, which might not always be practical.

Conclusion

Both the Black-Scholes and Binomial models are powerful tools for pricing options, each with its strengths and weaknesses. The Black-Scholes model is efficient and widely used for European options, while the Binomial model offers greater flexibility and accuracy for a broader range of options, including American options. Understanding these models allows traders to make more informed decisions, manage risk better, and develop more effective trading strategies in the complex world of options trading.

Alpha, Beta and the Capital Asset Pricing Model (CAPM)

In finance, alpha and beta are key metrics derived from the Capital Asset Pricing Model (CAPM), a fundamental model that describes the relationship between expected return and risk of an asset. CAPM serves as a cornerstone in modern portfolio theory, providing a framework to assess the risk-return tradeoff.

Capital Asset Pricing Model (CAPM)

The CAPM is based on the idea that investors need to be compensated in two ways: time value of money and risk. The model is expressed by the following equation:

$$E(R_i) = R_f + \beta_i \times (E(R_m) - R_f)$$

where:

- $E(R_i)$: Expected return of the asset
- R_f: Risk-free rate, typically represented by government bonds
- β_i: Asset's beta, a measure of its systematic risk
- $E(R_m)$: Expected return of the market
- $E(R_m) - R_f$: Market risk premium, the additional return expected for taking on market risk

CAPM assumes that all investors hold a combination of the risk-free asset and the market portfolio, which includes all risky assets in proportion to their market values. The model suggests that the expected return on an asset is determined by its beta, reflecting the asset's sensitivity to market movements, and the market risk premium, which compensates for taking on market risk.

While CAPM is widely used, it relies on several key assumptions:

- **Efficient Markets**: CAPM assumes that all investors have the same information and act rationally, leading to market efficiency.
- **Single Period Model**: CAPM is based on a single time period, often a year, making it less applicable for multi-period analysis.
- **Risk-Free Rate**: The model assumes the availability of a risk-free asset, which, in practice, may not perfectly exist.

One limitation of CAPM is its reliance on beta as the sole measure of risk, which ignores other factors like liquidity risk or default risk. Moreover, CAPM assumes that all investors hold the market portfolio, which is often impractical in reality.

Beta: Measuring Systematic Risk

Beta is a measure of an asset's systematic risk relative to the market as a whole. It indicates how much the asset's returns are expected to change in response to changes in the overall market. A beta of:

- **1** implies that the asset's price will move with the market.
- **Greater than 1** suggests the asset is more volatile than the market (e.g., technology stocks).
- **Less than 1** indicates the asset is less volatile than the market (e.g., utilities).

For example, if a stock has a beta of 1.3, and the market increases by 10%, the stock is expected to increase by 13%. Conversely, if the market falls by 10%, the stock is expected to decrease by 13%.

Beta helps investors understand the level of market risk associated with a particular asset, which is crucial for constructing a well-diversified portfolio. It captures only systematic risk, the risk inherent to the entire market or market segment, and excludes unsystematic risk, which is specific to an individual asset.

Alpha: Assessing Excess Return

Alpha represents the excess return of an asset or portfolio relative to the return predicted by CAPM, accounting for the asset's beta. It is calculated as:

$$\alpha = R_i - [R_f + \beta_i \times (R_m - R_f)]$$

Alpha is a measure of an investment's performance on a risk-adjusted basis. A positive alpha indicates that the asset has outperformed the expected return given its beta, suggesting that the asset or portfolio manager has added value. Conversely, a negative alpha indicates underperformance.

For instance, if an investor holds a stock with a beta of 1.1, and the market (expected to return 8%) indeed returns 8%, the CAPM would predict that the stock should return:

$$E(R_i) = 2\% + 1.1 \times (8\% - 2\%) = 8.6\%$$

If the actual return of the stock is 10%, the alpha is 1.4%, implying the stock has outperformed its expected return.

Practical Applications of CAPM, Alpha and Beta

- **Portfolio Construction**: Investors use beta to balance portfolios according to their risk tolerance. For example, a conservative investor might seek assets with lower betas to reduce exposure to market fluctuations.
- **Performance Evaluation**: Alpha is crucial in evaluating the performance of mutual funds and portfolio managers. A consistently positive alpha suggests that a manager can generate returns above the expected market level, after adjusting for risk.
- **Risk Management**: CAPM and beta are employed in risk management strategies to estimate potential losses in adverse market conditions and to adjust portfolio positions accordingly.

DOWNSIDE DEVIATION

Downside Deviation is a risk metric that quantifies the volatility of negative returns or deviations below a minimum acceptable return (MAR), typically set at zero. This measure is particularly relevant in assessing investments that involve income strategies, such as options trading, where the primary concern is often the potential for losses rather than the overall volatility.

Defining Downside Deviation

Downside Deviation is a variation of standard deviation but focuses solely on the negative side of returns. Unlike the standard deviation, which considers both positive and negative deviations from the mean, downside deviation isolates the standard deviation of returns that fall below a predefined threshold. This threshold is often set at zero or another specified minimum acceptable return.

The formula for calculating Downside Deviation is:

$$\text{Downside Deviation} = \sqrt{\frac{\sum_{i=1}^{N} \max(0, MAR - R_i)^2}{N}}$$

where:

- MAR is the Minimum Acceptable Return,
- R_i represents the returns below the MAR,
- N is the number of observations.

Downside Deviation is crucial in financial analysis for several reasons:

- **Focus on Negative Risk:** It emphasizes the risk of underperformance rather than the overall volatility. This is particularly relevant for risk-averse investors who are more concerned with avoiding losses than with the overall variability of returns.
- **Improved Risk Assessment:** By concentrating on returns that fall below the acceptable threshold, Downside Deviation provides a more accurate measure of risk for strategies where negative outcomes are more impactful, such as in income-focused strategies using covered calls and cash-secured puts.

Implications for Option Income Strategies

For investors using option income strategies like covered calls and cash-secured puts, Downside Deviation provides a focused measure of potential risk. Strategies involving options can experience substantial variations in performance due to market fluctuations and the nature of option pricing.

By evaluating Downside Deviation, investors can better understand and manage the risk of underperformance relative to their threshold for acceptable returns.

- **Risk Management:** Investors can use Downside Deviation to evaluate how well their strategies protect against negative outcomes, tailoring their approach to minimize downside risk.
- **Performance Comparison:** Comparing the Downside Deviation of different strategies or assets can help investors select those with lower potential for significant losses.

In summary, Downside Deviation is a vital metric for assessing risk in investment strategies, particularly those focused on generating income where minimizing the risk of losses is paramount. By focusing on deviations below a minimum acceptable return, it offers a nuanced view of risk that complements other volatility measures.

GLOSSARY

A

Alpha: Alpha measures the excess return of an investment relative to the return predicted by the CAPM or another benchmark. It reflects the performance of an asset or portfolio after accounting for market-related risks. A positive alpha indicates that the investment has outperformed its expected return, suggesting effective management or superior asset selection.

American Option: An American option is an options contract that can be exercised at any time before or on the expiration date. This flexibility allows the holder to take advantage of favorable movements in the underlying asset's price at any point during the life of the option. American options are commonly used for stocks and ETFs, providing opportunities for early exercise, such as when a stock pays a dividend.

Anchoring: Anchoring is a cognitive bias where an individual relies too heavily on the first piece of information encountered when making decisions. In trading, this can affect how investors assess the value of assets or set price targets.

Asset Class: An asset class is a category of financial assets with similar characteristics, such as stocks, bonds, commodities, or real estate. Different asset classes typically have different risk and return profiles.

At the Money (ATM): An option is "at the money" when the underlying asset's price is equal to the option's strike price. In this case, the option has no intrinsic value but may still have time value.

Autocorrelation Function (ACF): The Autocorrelation Function (ACF) measures the correlation between a time series and a lagged version of itself. It quantifies how current values of the series are related to past values at different time lags. This function is crucial for identifying patterns and seasonality in time series data. For example, in stock price analysis, a significant autocorrelation at a lag of 12 months might indicate annual seasonal effects.

B

Beta: Beta is a measure of an asset's sensitivity to market movements, capturing its systematic risk. It quantifies how much an asset's returns are expected to change in response to market fluctuations. A beta of 1 implies that the asset moves with the market, while a beta greater or less than 1 indicates higher or lower volatility relative to the market, respectively.

Bid-Ask Spread: The bid-ask spread is the difference between the highest price a buyer is willing to pay (bid) and the lowest price a seller is willing to accept (ask) for a security. It represents the cost of liquidity in the market. A narrower spread indicates a more liquid market, while a wider spread suggests lower liquidity and higher transaction costs.

Binomial Model: The binomial model is an option pricing model that uses a tree of possible future prices for the underlying asset to estimate the option's value. It accounts for multiple time periods and possible outcomes.

Black-Litterman Model: The Black-Litterman model is an asset allocation model that combines market equilibrium with investor views to generate more stable and diversified portfolios. It is used to improve the robustness of portfolio construction.

Black-Scholes Model: The Black-Scholes model is a mathematical model used to estimate the fair value of options. It considers factors such as the underlying asset's price, volatility, time to expiration, and interest rates to calculate the option's price.

Blue-Chip Stock: A blue-chip stock is a stock of a large, well-established, and financially stable company with a history of reliable earnings and dividend payments. Blue-chip stocks are typically considered low-risk investments.

Bollinger Bands: Bollinger Bands are technical analysis tools that plot an asset's price within bands based on its moving average and standard deviation. They are used to assess volatility and identify potential reversal points.

Book Value per Share: Book value per share is calculated by dividing a company's total equity by the number of outstanding shares. It represents the value of a company's net assets on a per-share basis and is used as a measure of intrinsic value. Investors use it to assess whether a stock is under- or overvalued relative to its book value.

Breakeven Point: The breakeven point is the underlying asset price at which the options strategy results in neither profit nor loss. It is calculated by factoring in the premiums received or paid.

Broker: A broker is a financial intermediary that facilitates the buying and selling of financial instruments, such as stocks, bonds, and options, on behalf of clients. Brokers may also provide advice and research services.

Buying Power: Buying power is the total amount of capital available to a trader for opening new positions, considering both cash and margin. It determines the maximum size of trades that can be executed.

C

Call: A call option grants the holder the right to buy an underlying asset at a specified strike price within a specified period. The seller of the call option has the obligation to sell the asset if the buyer exercises the option.

Call Ratio Spread: A call ratio spread involves buying a certain number of call options and selling a larger number of call options with the same expiration date but a different strike price. It is a neutral to bullish strategy.

Capital Asset Pricing Model (CAPM): The Capital Asset Pricing Model (CAPM) is a financial model that describes the relationship between systematic risk and expected return for assets, particularly stocks. It is used to estimate the cost of equity.

Capital Expenditures (CapEx): CapEx refers to the funds used by a company to acquire, upgrade, or maintain physical assets such as property, plant, and equipment. CapEx is essential for sustaining and growing a company's operations but represents a significant cash outflow. Analysts monitor CapEx to assess a company's investment in its future growth and its impact on free cash flow.

Capital Market Line (CML): The Capital Market Line (CML) represents the risk-return tradeoff in a market where all investors have identical expectations and can borrow or lend at the risk-free rate. It shows the optimal portfolio of risky assets combined with the risk-free asset.

Capital Requirement: Capital requirement refers to the amount of funds that must be reserved to cover the potential obligations of an options strategy, such as the cost of buying the underlying asset or margin requirements.

Capital Reserve: A capital reserve is a portion of a trader's capital set aside to cover potential losses. It provides a financial cushion for the trader.

Cash-Secured Put: A cash-secured put involves selling a put option while holding enough cash to purchase the underlying asset if the option is exercised. This strategy generates income from the premium while being prepared to buy the asset at the strike price.

Cash Settlement: Cash settlement is a method of settling an options contract by paying the cash difference between the strike price and the market price of the underlying asset, rather than delivering the physical asset. This is common in index options, where it is impractical to deliver the underlying assets. Upon exercise, the option holder receives a cash amount equal to the profit they would have made if the option were physically settled.

Central Banks: Central banks are national financial institutions responsible for managing a country's monetary policy, regulating banks, and maintaining financial stability. They influence interest rates, control inflation, and implement policies to stabilize the economy. Notable examples include the Federal Reserve (Fed) in the United States and the European Central Bank (ECB) in the Eurozone.

Collar: A collar is an options strategy that involves holding a long position in an asset, buying a protective put, and selling a covered call. It limits both the upside and downside potential, providing a balanced risk-reward profile.

Commodity: A commodity is a raw material or primary agricultural product that can be bought and sold, such as oil, gold, or wheat. Commodities are traded on specialized markets and are subject to supply and demand fluctuations.

Commodity Futures Trading (CFT): Commodity Futures Trading (CFT) involves buying and selling futures contracts for commodities such as oil, gold, or agricultural products. Futures contracts are agreements to buy or sell a commodity at a predetermined price on a specified future date. This trading helps manage price risk and speculate on future price movements.

Confidence Interval: A confidence interval is a range of values derived from a data set that is likely to contain the true population parameter with a specified level of confidence, such as 95%.

Consumer Confidence Index (CCI): The Consumer Confidence Index (CCI) measures the degree of optimism that consumers feel about the overall state of the economy and their personal financial situation. It is a leading economic indicator that can predict consumer spending patterns, which in turn affects economic growth. A rising CCI typically signals increased consumer spending and economic expansion.

Consumer Price Index (CPI): The Consumer Price Index (CPI) tracks changes in the average prices paid by consumers for a basket of goods and services over time. It is a key indicator of inflation, reflecting the cost of living and purchasing power. Central banks use CPI to adjust monetary policy to maintain price stability.

Correlation: Correlation is a statistical measure that indicates the degree to which two assets move in relation to each other. A positive correlation means they move in the same direction, while a negative correlation means they move in opposite directions.

Correlation Matrix: A correlation matrix is a table showing the correlation coefficients between multiple assets. It helps in understanding the relationships between different assets and is used in portfolio optimization.

Covariance: Covariance is a measure of how two variables change together. In finance, it is used to assess how the returns of two assets move relative to each other, helping in portfolio diversification.

Covered Call: A covered call strategy involves holding a long position in an underlying asset and selling a call option on the same asset. It generates income from the option premium while potentially capping the upside.

Credit Risk: Credit risk is the risk of loss arising from a borrower or counterparty's failure to meet their contractual obligations. It is a key consideration in lending and derivatives markets.

Cumulative Distribution Function (CDF): The Cumulative Distribution Function (CDF) of a random variable X is a function $F_X(x)$ that describes the probability that X will take a value less than or equal to x.

Cyclical Sectors: Cyclical sectors include industries that are highly sensitive to economic cycles, with performance closely tied to the overall health of the economy. Companies in these sectors, such as consumer discretionary, industrials, materials, financials, and real estate, tend to perform well during economic expansions and suffer during recessions.

D

Debt to Equity (D/E) Ratio: The D/E ratio is a financial leverage metric that compares a company's total debt to its shareholders' equity. It indicates the proportion of financing that comes from debt versus equity. A higher D/E ratio suggests greater financial risk, as the company relies more on borrowed funds. Conversely, a lower ratio indicates a more conservative capital structure.

Defensive Sectors: Defensive sectors consist of industries that are less sensitive to economic cycles and tend to perform relatively well during economic downturns. These sectors, such as consumer staples, healthcare, and utilities, provide essential goods and services that remain in demand regardless of economic conditions.

Delta: Delta measures the sensitivity of an option's price to changes in the price of the underlying asset. It ranges from 0 to 1 for calls and from 0 to -1 for puts, indicating the probability of the option being in the money at expiration.

Delta Hedging: Delta hedging is a risk management strategy used in options trading that involves adjusting the position in the underlying asset to offset changes in the option's delta. Delta represents the sensitivity of an option's price to changes in the price of the underlying asset. By frequently adjusting the position, the trader aims to maintain a delta-neutral portfolio, reducing exposure to price movements in the underlying asset.

Distribution: Distribution in finance and statistics refers to the way values, such as returns, prices, or other data points, are spread or dispersed over a range. In the context of financial markets, distribution often describes how the returns of an asset are spread across different possible outcomes, typically visualized in a histogram or a probability density function.

Diversification (Portfolio): Diversification is the practice of spreading investments across various asset classes, sectors, or instruments to reduce risk. A diversified portfolio is less likely to suffer large losses from the poor performance of a single asset.

Dividend: A dividend is a portion of a company's earnings distributed to shareholders, typically in the form of cash or additional shares. Dividends are a key component of total return for investors and can signal a company's financial health and stability. The dividend yield, calculated as the annual dividend per share divided by the share price, indicates the income generated by holding the stock.

Dividend Yield: Dividend yield is a financial ratio that indicates the annual dividend income received from a stock relative to its current price. It is a measure of the income generated from an investment in a stock.

Dividend-Paying Stock: A dividend-paying stock is a stock of a company that regularly distributes a portion of its earnings to shareholders in the form of dividends. These stocks are often favored by income-focused investors.

Double Down: Double down is an aggressive trading strategy where a trader increases their position size in a losing trade to average down the entry price, aiming for a larger profit when the market reverses.

Downside Deviation: Downside deviation is a measure of the variability of returns that fall below a specified threshold, typically the risk-free rate or a target return. Unlike standard deviation, which considers all volatility, downside deviation focuses only on negative returns. It is used in performance evaluation and risk management to assess the extent of potential losses and the likelihood of not meeting investment objectives.

Drawdown: Drawdown is the peak-to-trough decline in the value of a trading account or investment. It measures the amount of loss before a new peak is achieved, reflecting the risk of a trading strategy.

E

Earnings per Share (EPS): EPS measures a company's profitability by dividing its net income by the number of outstanding shares. It represents the portion of a company's profit allocated to each share of stock and is a key indicator of financial performance. Higher EPS typically indicates greater profitability and is often used to compare companies within the same industry.

Economic Cycle: The Economic Cycle refers to the natural rise and fall of economic growth over time. It includes four phases: Expansion (increasing economic activity), Peak (the height of economic activity), Contraction (a decline in economic activity), and Trough (the lowest point of economic activity before recovery begins).

Efficient Frontier: The efficient frontier is a line on a risk-return graph representing the set of optimal portfolios that offer the highest expected return for a given level of risk. Portfolios on the efficient frontier are considered well-diversified.

Equity: Equity represents ownership in a company, typically in the form of stocks. It entitles the holder to a share of the company's assets and earnings and may also include voting rights.

ETF (Exchange-Traded Fund): An ETF is a type of investment fund that is traded on stock exchanges, much like stocks. It holds a collection of assets, such as stocks, bonds, or commodities, and allows investors to diversify their holdings.

European Central Bank (ECB): The European Central Bank (ECB) is the central bank for the Eurozone, responsible for monetary policy within the Euro area. Its main objectives include maintaining price stability, managing interest rates, and regulating financial institutions to ensure economic stability.

European Option: A European option is a type of options contract that can only be exercised on its expiration date. Unlike American options, which can be exercised at any time before expiration, European options restrict the exercise of the option to a single point in time. These options are often used in financial markets for index options and other instruments where early exercise is not typically necessary.

European Securities and Markets Authority (ESMA): The European Securities and Markets Authority (ESMA) is a European Union regulatory agency responsible for improving the functioning of financial markets and enhancing investor protection. It oversees securities markets, ensures transparency, and enforces regulations across the EU.

Event Risk: Event risk arises from unforeseen events such as geopolitical tensions, economic crises, or corporate scandals that can dramatically impact financial markets, leading to sharp movements in asset prices.

Expectancy: Expectancy refers to the expected average outcome of a trading strategy over time, calculated by considering both the probability of success and the potential rewards and losses.

Expected Loss: Expected loss is the anticipated average loss from a trading strategy, considering the likelihood of losing trades and the size of those losses. It is a key metric in risk management.

F

Federal Open Market Committee (FOMC): The Federal Open Market Committee (FOMC) is a component of the Federal Reserve that oversees open market operations and sets monetary policy. It meets regularly to review economic conditions and make decisions on interest rates and other monetary policies to influence economic growth and inflation.

Federal Reserve (FED): The Federal Reserve, or Fed, is the central banking system of the United States. It is responsible for conducting monetary policy, supervising and regulating banks, maintaining financial stability, and providing financial services. It influences interest rates and money supply to promote economic stability.

Financial Services Authority (FSA): The Financial Services Authority (FSA) was a regulatory body in the UK responsible for regulating financial services and markets. It was replaced by the Financial Conduct Authority (FCA) and the Prudential Regulation Authority (PRA) in 2013. It aimed to protect consumers, maintain market integrity, and promote competition.

FOMO (Fear of Missing Out): FOMO is a psychological phenomenon where traders or investors feel compelled to enter a trade or investment out of fear of missing out on potential profits. It can lead to impulsive and irrational decision-making.

Fourier Analysis: Fourier Analysis is a mathematical method used to analyze and decompose time series data into its frequency components. By transforming a time series from the time domain to the frequency domain, Fourier Analysis helps identify cyclical patterns and periodicities in the data.

Free Cash Flow (FCF): FCF represents the cash generated by a company after accounting for capital expenditures necessary to maintain or expand its asset base. It is a key indicator of financial flexibility and the ability to generate shareholder value. Positive FCF allows a company to invest in growth, pay dividends, reduce debt, or repurchase shares.

G

Gamma: Gamma measures the rate of change of delta with respect to changes in the underlying asset's price. It reflects the convexity of the option's price and indicates the stability of the delta.

Gamma Scalping: Gamma scalping is a dynamic hedging strategy used in options trading to manage the gamma risk of an options position. Gamma measures the rate of change in an option's delta as the underlying asset price moves. By frequently adjusting the position in the underlying asset, traders aim to maintain a delta-neutral position and capture profits from price movements while managing the risks associated with gamma exposure.

Gross Domestic Product (GDP): Gross Domestic Product (GDP) measures the total value of goods and services produced within a country's borders over a specific period. It is a key indicator of economic performance and growth. Rising GDP typically indicates economic expansion, while falling GDP may signal a recession.

Growth Stock: A growth stock is a stock of a company expected to grow at an above-average rate compared to other companies in the market. Growth stocks typically do not pay dividends, as profits are reinvested into the company.

H

Hedging: Hedging is a risk management strategy used to offset potential losses in an investment by taking an opposing position in a related asset, such as using options to protect against adverse price movements in a stock.

Historical Distribution: Historical distribution refers to the frequency distribution of past returns or prices of an asset. It helps in understanding the asset's historical behavior and estimating future performance.

Historical Volatility: Historical volatility measures the past price fluctuations of an asset over a specific period. It is calculated as the standard deviation of returns and provides insight into the asset's past price behavior.

I

Implied Volatility: Implied volatility is a forward-looking measure derived from the option's market price. It reflects the market's expectations of future price fluctuations of the underlying asset.

Implied Volatility Percentile (IV Percentile): Implied Volatility Percentile measures the percentage of time that the implied volatility has been below the current level over a specific period, typically a year. A higher percentile indicates relatively high implied volatility.

Implied Volatility Rank (IV Rank): Implied Volatility Rank compares the current implied volatility of an asset to its range over a specific period, usually a year. It indicates whether the current IV is high or low relative to its historical values.

In the Money (ITM): An option is "in the money" when exercising it would lead to a positive cash flow. For a call option, this means the underlying asset's price is above the strike price. For a put option, it means the asset's price is below the strike price.

Index: An index is a statistical measure that tracks the performance of a group of assets, such as stocks or bonds, representing a specific market or sector. Indices are used as benchmarks for portfolio performance.

Interest Cost: Interest cost is the expense incurred from borrowing funds to finance a leveraged position. It reduces the net return on leveraged trades and must be considered in margin trading.

Intrinsic Value: Intrinsic value is the value of an option if it were exercised immediately. It is the difference between the underlying asset's price and the option's strike price, provided it is favorable to the option holder.

Inverted Strangle: An inverted strangle involves selling an in-the-money call and put, with the put having a higher strike price than the call.

Iron Butterfly: Iron Butterfly is risk-defined options strategy that involves four options contracts, typically using the same expiration date. The strategy combines elements of both a straddle (short) and a strangle (long) and is designed to profit from low volatility and minimal movement in the underlying asset's price.

Iron Condor: An iron condor is an options strategy that involves selling an out-of-the-money call and put, while simultaneously buying a further out-of-the-money call and put. It is a neutral strategy that profits from low volatility.

K

Kelly Criterion: The Kelly Criterion is a mathematical formula used to determine the optimal size of a series of bets or trades to maximize long-term growth while managing risk. It is based on the probability of success and the ratio of wins to losses.

L

Large-Cap: Large-cap stocks refer to shares of companies with a market capitalization typically above $10 billion. These companies are often well-established, with stable revenue streams and a significant presence in their industries. Large-cap stocks are generally considered less volatile and offer more predictable returns than smaller companies.

LEAPS Option (Long-Term Equity Anticipation Security): LEAPS are long-term options, typically with expiration dates longer than one year, that provide extended exposure to the underlying asset. They are used for long-term speculation or hedging.

Leverage: Leverage involves using borrowed funds or margin to increase the potential return of an investment. It amplifies both profits and losses, making it a high-risk, high-reward strategy.

Liabilities: Total liabilities encompass all financial obligations a company owes to external parties, including short-term and long-term debt, accounts payable, and other liabilities. It is a key component of a company's balance sheet and is used in conjunction with total assets to assess financial stability and leverage.

Liquidity: Liquidity refers to the ease with which an asset can be bought or sold in the market without affecting its price. High liquidity ensures efficient market functioning and tighter bid-ask spreads.

Liquidity Risk: Liquidity risk is the risk that an asset cannot be bought or sold quickly enough in the market without significantly affecting its price, leading to potential losses or the inability to execute trades.

Loss Aversion: Loss aversion is a behavioral finance concept that describes the tendency of individuals to prefer avoiding losses rather than acquiring equivalent gains. It can lead to suboptimal decision-making in trading.

M

MACD (Moving Average Convergence Divergence): MACD is a momentum indicator that shows the relationship between two moving averages of an asset's price. It helps identify trends, potential buy/sell signals, and changes in momentum.

Manufacturing Purchasing Managers' Index (PMI): The Manufacturing Purchasing Managers' Index (PMI) is an economic indicator derived from surveys of manufacturing executives. It measures the health of the manufacturing sector, including factors such as production levels, new orders, and employment. A PMI above 50 indicates expansion, while below 50 indicates contraction.

Margin Call: A margin call occurs when a trader's account equity falls below the required margin level, prompting the broker to demand additional funds or the liquidation of positions to restore the margin balance.

Margin Requirement: Margin requirement refers to the minimum amount of equity that must be maintained in a margin account when holding leveraged positions. It is set by the broker or regulatory bodies and varies by asset type.

Market Cap: Market capitalization, or market cap, is the total value of a company's outstanding shares of stock. It is calculated by multiplying the current stock price by the total number of outstanding shares. Market cap is used to classify companies into different categories, such as large-cap, mid-cap, and small-cap, which helps investors assess a company's size and market value.

Market Risk: Market risk refers to the potential for losses due to factors that affect the overall performance of financial markets, such as economic changes, interest rates, and geopolitical events.

Mean: The mean is the average of a data set, calculated by summing all the values and dividing by the number of observations. It is a measure of central tendency.

Median: The median is the middle value in a data set when the values are arranged in ascending or descending order. It represents the 50th percentile and is less affected by outliers than the mean.

Micro-Cap: Micro-cap stocks refer to companies with a market capitalization between approximately 50 million and 300 million. These stocks are often associated with higher risk and volatility due to their smaller size and limited liquidity, but they can offer significant growth potential.

Mid-Cap: Mid-cap stocks are shares of companies with a market capitalization ranging from approximately 2 billion to 10 billion. These companies are usually in a growth phase, offering a balance between stability and potential for higher returns. Mid-cap stocks can be more volatile than large-cap stocks but often provide greater growth opportunities.

Mode: The mode is the value that appears most frequently in a data set. It is a measure of central tendency that indicates the most common observation.

Modern Portfolio Theory (MPT): Modern Portfolio Theory (MPT) is an investment framework that emphasizes the importance of diversification to optimize portfolio returns for a given level of risk. It introduces the concept of the efficient frontier.

Monte Carlo Simulation: Monte Carlo Simulation is a statistical technique that uses random sampling to model the probability of different outcomes in a complex system. It is used in finance to estimate the range of potential future returns.

Moving Averages: Moving Averages are statistical tools used to smooth out fluctuations in time series data and identify trends. They are calculated by averaging data points over a specific period. Common types include Simple Moving Averages (SMA) and Exponential Moving Averages (EMA), each serving different purposes in trend analysis.

N

Nano-Cap: Nano-cap stocks are the smallest publicly traded companies, with market capitalizations typically below $50 million. These stocks are highly speculative and volatile, with limited liquidity, making them risky investments but potentially rewarding for those seeking high-risk, high-reward opportunities.

Non-Farm Payrolls (NFP): Non-Farm Payrolls (NFP) refer to the number of jobs added or lost in the U.S. economy, excluding farm workers, government employees, and some other sectors. It is a key monthly indicator of economic health and employment trends, influencing market expectations and central bank policies.

Normal Distribution: A normal distribution is a statistical distribution where data points are symmetrically distributed around the mean, forming a bell-shaped curve. It is used in finance to model returns and assess probabilities.

O

Open Interest: Open interest refers to the total number of outstanding derivative contracts, such as options or futures, that have not been settled. It is a measure of market activity and liquidity, with higher open interest indicating a more active and liquid market. Open interest is used to gauge the strength of a market trend and potential price movements.

Operating Cash Flow (OCF): OCF measures the cash generated by a company's core operating activities, excluding capital expenditures. It reflects the company's ability to generate sufficient cash flow to sustain operations and fund day-to-day activities. OCF is a critical indicator of a company's financial health and operational efficiency.

Operational Risk: Operational risk involves losses resulting from failures in internal processes, systems, or controls. This includes technical issues, human errors, or system outages that can impact trading execution and strategy implementation.

Option: An option is a financial derivative that gives the holder the right, but not the obligation, to buy (call) or sell (put) an underlying asset at a specified strike price before or on a specified expiration date. Options are used for hedging, speculation, and income generation.

Option Adjustments: Option adjustments involve modifying an existing options position to manage risk, improve returns, or respond to market conditions. Adjustments may include rolling, adding or closing positions.

Option Expiration Date: The option expiration date is the last date on which the option can be exercised. After this date, the option expires and becomes worthless if not exercised.

Option Premium: The option premium is the price paid by the buyer to the seller for the rights conferred by the option. It consists of the intrinsic value and the time value of the option.

Option Time Value: Option time value represents the portion of the option premium that exceeds its intrinsic value. It reflects the potential for the option to gain value before expiration due to market movements.

Out of the Money (OTM): An option is "out of the money" when exercising it would not be profitable. For a call option, this occurs when the underlying asset's price is below the strike price. For a put option, it happens when the asset's price is above the strike price.

P

Paper Trading: Paper trading involves simulated trading in a risk-free environment using virtual money. It allows traders to practice strategies and gain experience without risking real capital.

Payoff: The payoff is the profit or loss realized from holding an option at expiration or after exercising it. It depends on the difference between the strike price and the underlying asset's market price.

Penny Stocks: Penny stocks refer to shares of small, often speculative companies that trade at low prices, typically under $5 per share. These stocks are highly volatile and risky, with limited liquidity and a higher likelihood of price manipulation, but they can offer substantial returns if the company succeeds.

Percentile: A percentile is a measure used to indicate the value below which a given percentage of observations fall in a data set. It is used in statistical analysis to compare relative standing.

Personal Consumption Expenditure (PCE): Personal Consumption Expenditure (PCE) measures the changes in the prices of goods and services consumed by households. It is a key indicator of inflation and consumer spending. The Federal Reserve closely monitors the PCE index to guide monetary policy decisions.

Physical Settlement: Physical settlement refers to the process of fulfilling an options contract by delivering the actual underlying asset. When an option is exercised, the seller (writer) of the option must deliver the physical asset, such as stocks, bonds, or commodities, to the buyer. For example, if a call option on a stock is exercised, the seller must deliver the specified number of shares to the buyer at the agreed-upon strike price.

Position Sizing: Position sizing is the process of determining how much capital to allocate to a single trade based on the risk involved and the overall trading strategy. Proper position sizing helps manage risk by ensuring that no single trade can significantly impact the portfolio.

Post-Modern Portfolio Theory (PMPT): Post-Modern Portfolio Theory (PMPT) is an extension of MPT that focuses on downside risk and investor preferences. It incorporates measures like the Sortino ratio to better reflect investor concerns about losses.

Potential Loss: Potential loss refers to the possible loss that can occur from an options strategy.

Pre-Market / After-Hours Trading: Pre-Market and After-Hours Trading refer to the trading of securities outside the regular market hours. Pre-Market Trading occurs before the market opens, while After-Hours Trading happens after the market closes. These sessions allow investors to react to news and events that occur outside normal trading hours.

Price to Book (P/B) Ratio: The P/B ratio compares a company's market value to its book value, calculated as the market price per share divided by the book value per share. It reflects how much investors are willing to pay for each dollar of net assets. A P/B ratio greater than 1 suggests that the market values the company more than its book value, often due to expectations of future growth.

Price to Earnings (P/E) Ratio: The P/E ratio is a valuation metric that compares a company's current share price to its earnings per share (EPS). It indicates how much investors are willing to pay for each dollar of earnings. A high P/E ratio may suggest that the stock is overvalued or that investors expect high growth in the future, while a low P/E ratio may indicate undervaluation.

Probability Density Function (PDF): The Probability Density Function (PDF) of a continuous random variable X is a function $f_X(x)$ that describes the likelihood of X taking a specific value x.

Probability of Touching: The probability of touching refers to the likelihood that the underlying asset's price will reach or exceed a specific strike price at least once during the option's life. It is generally higher than the probability of the option being in the money at expiration.

Put: A put option gives the holder the right to sell an underlying asset at a predetermined strike price within a specified timeframe. The seller of the put option is obliged to purchase the asset if the option is exercised.

Put Ratio Spread: A put ratio spread involves buying a certain number of put options and selling a larger number of put options with the same expiration date but a different strike price. It is a neutral to bearish strategy.

R

Recency Bias: Recency bias is a cognitive bias where individuals give undue weight to recent events or experiences when making decisions. In trading, this can lead to overestimating the importance of short-term market movements.

Regression Analysis with Seasonal Dummies: Regression Analysis with Seasonal Dummies involves incorporating dummy variables representing different seasons or months into a regression model. This technique helps quantify and control for seasonal effects on a time series, improving the accuracy of forecasts and understanding seasonal impacts on the dependent variable.

Retail Sales: Retail Sales measure the total receipts of retail stores, reflecting consumer spending patterns. It is a key economic indicator that provides insights into consumer confidence and economic health. An increase in retail sales suggests higher consumer spending and economic growth.

Return (Daily): Daily return is the percentage change in the value of an asset from one day to the next. It is a key metric for measuring short-term performance and calculating volatility.

Rho: Rho measures the sensitivity of an option's price to changes in interest rates. It indicates how much the option's price will change for a 1% change in interest rates.

Risk Parity: Risk parity is a portfolio construction strategy that allocates capital based on the risk contribution of each asset, rather than allocating based on expected returns or capital alone. The goal is to equalize the risk across different asset classes, achieving a more balanced and diversified portfolio. This method often involves leveraging lower-risk assets to equalize risk exposure across the portfolio.

Rolling (Option) Up/Down/Out: Rolling an option involves closing an existing position and opening a new one with a different strike price or expiration date. Rolling up or down adjusts the strike price, while rolling out extends the expiration date.

S

Seasonal Autoregressive Integrated Moving Average (SARIMA): Seasonal Autoregressive Integrated Moving Average (SARIMA) Is a time series forecasting model that extends the ARIMA model by including seasonal components. It accounts for both non-seasonal and seasonal patterns in data, making it suitable for forecasting with strong seasonal effects.

Seasonal Decomposition of Time Series by LOESS (STL): Seasonal Decomposition of Time Series by LOESS (STL) is a method for decomposing a time series into its trend, seasonal, and residual components using locally weighted regression (LOESS). STL is flexible and can handle any type of seasonality and trend, providing a robust decomposition of the time series.

Seasonal Subseries Plot: A Seasonal Subseries Plot is a graphical tool used to visualize seasonal patterns within a time series. It displays data for each season (e.g., month) across multiple years in separate subplots. This visualization helps identify recurring seasonal trends and variations.

Securities and Exchange Commission (SEC): The Securities and Exchange Commission (SEC) is the U.S. regulatory agency responsible for overseeing securities markets and protecting investors. It enforces federal securities laws, regulates stock exchanges, and ensures fair and transparent trading practices.

Sector: An economic sector refers to a large segment of the economy that is made up of companies and industries with similar business activities. Sectors are often used to categorize companies for investment analysis. Common sectors include Technology, Healthcare, Financials, Energy, and Consumer Discretionary.

Sensitive Sectors: Sensitive sectors include industries that have moderate correlations with business cycles. These sectors, such as technology, energy, and communication services, are influenced by economic conditions but may not be as directly tied to the business cycle as cyclical sectors

Sensitivity Analysis: Sensitivity analysis in option trading involves evaluating how the price or risk metrics of an option or a portfolio of options respond to changes in underlying factors such as the price of the underlying asset, implied volatility, interest rates, or time to expiration.

Sharpe Ratio: The Sharpe Ratio measures the risk-adjusted return of an investment by comparing the excess return (over the risk-free rate) to its standard deviation. It is a key metric for evaluating the performance of a portfolio, with a higher Sharpe Ratio indicating better risk-adjusted returns. The ratio helps investors assess whether an investment's returns justify its risk.

Short Selling: Short selling involves selling an asset that the seller does not own, typically by borrowing it, with the intention of buying it back later at a lower price to make a profit.

Short Straddle: A short straddle involves selling both a call and a put option at the same strike price and expiration date. The strategy profits from low volatility and the expectation that the underlying asset will remain at or near the strike price.

Short Strangle: A short strangle involves selling an out-of-the-money call and put with the same expiration date. The strategy profits from low volatility and the expectation that the underlying asset will remain within a certain price range.

Simple Moving Average (SMA): A Simple Moving Average (SMA) is a technical analysis tool used to smooth out price data by creating a constantly updated average price over a specified period. The SMA is calculated by adding the closing prices of an asset over a set number of periods and then dividing the total by the number of periods.

Small-Cap: Small-cap stocks are shares of companies with a market capitalization between approximately 300 million and 2 billion. These companies are typically in the early stages of growth and can offer high potential returns but also come with increased risk and volatility.

Sortino Ratio: The Sortino Ratio is a variation of the Sharpe Ratio that focuses on downside risk by considering only the standard deviation of negative returns. It measures the risk-adjusted return relative to a target or minimum acceptable return, providing a more accurate assessment of performance for investments with asymmetric return distributions or significant downside risks.

Standard Deviation: Standard deviation is a statistical measure of the dispersion of returns around the mean. It quantifies the level of risk or volatility of an asset's price.

Stock: A stock represents ownership in a corporation and constitutes a claim on part of the company's assets and earnings. Stocks are traded on stock exchanges and are a fundamental component of investment portfolios.

Stock Repair Strategy: The stock repair strategy involves using options to reduce the break-even point on a losing stock position without additional capital investment. Typically, this is done by buying and selling call options to offset losses.

Stop Loss: A stop-loss is an order placed to sell a security when it reaches a certain price level, used to limit potential losses in a position. It is a key tool in risk management.

Stress Testing: Stress testing in option trading is the process of assessing how an option or portfolio of options would perform under extreme or adverse market conditions. This involves simulating various scenarios, such as significant price movements in the underlying asset, drastic changes in implied volatility, or sudden shifts in interest rates. The goal of stress testing is to identify potential vulnerabilities and to evaluate the potential impact on profitability and risk exposure.

Strike Price: The strike price is the price at which the holder of an option can buy (call) or sell (put) the underlying asset. It is a key determinant in the option's value and the decision to exercise.

Symmetry (Distribution): Distribution symmetry refers to the degree to which the values in a data set are evenly distributed around the mean. A perfectly symmetric distribution has equal values on both sides of the mean.

T

Tail Risk: Tail risk refers to the probability of rare, extreme events occurring that could cause significant losses in a portfolio. These events fall in the "tails" of the normal distribution curve of returns, hence the name. Managing tail risk often involves strategies such as buying options or other derivatives that increase in value during extreme market movements.

Theta: Theta represents the rate of time decay of an option. It quantifies how much the option's price decreases as the expiration date approaches, all else being equal.

Ticker: A ticker is a unique symbol or series of letters assigned to a publicly traded asset, such as a stock or ETF, to identify it on an exchange. Tickers are used to track prices and trades in the financial markets.

Time Decay (Theta): Time decay, measured by the option's theta, refers to the gradual decrease in the value of an option as it approaches its expiration date.

It reflects the diminishing time value of the option.

Trading Plan: A trading plan is a documented set of rules and guidelines that a trader follows when executing trades. It includes criteria for entering and exiting trades, risk management strategies, and performance evaluation.

Transaction Costs: Transaction costs are expenses incurred when buying or selling securities. These costs include broker commissions, bid-ask spreads, and other fees associated with trading. Transaction costs can significantly impact investment returns, particularly for high-frequency trading strategies, and must be considered when evaluating the overall profitability of trades.

U

Underlying Asset (of an Option): The underlying asset is the financial instrument (e.g., stock, index, ETF) on which an option contract is based. The value and performance of the option are directly tied to the underlying asset.

Unemployment: Unemployment measures the percentage of the labor force that is actively seeking employment but is unable to find work. It is a critical economic indicator that reflects the health of the labor market and overall economic conditions. High unemployment rates can signal economic distress, while low rates typically indicate a robust job market.

V

Value at Risk (VaR): Value at Risk (VaR) is a risk management metric that estimates the maximum potential loss of a portfolio over a specific period, given a certain confidence level. It is used to assess the risk of extreme losses.

Value Stock: Value stocks are shares of companies that appear to be undervalued relative to their fundamentals, such as earnings, dividends, or sales. These stocks trade at a lower price than their intrinsic value, making them attractive to investors seeking to capitalize on potential price appreciation when the market recognizes the stock's true value.

Variance: Variance measures the dispersion of returns around the mean return, indicating the level of risk or uncertainty associated with an asset's price movements. It is the square of the standard deviation.

Vega: Vega measures the sensitivity of an option's price to changes in implied volatility. Higher vega implies greater sensitivity to volatility changes, which impacts the option's premium.

Vertical Credit Spread (Call / Put): A vertical credit spread involves selling an option and buying another option of the same type (call or put) with a different strike price but the same expiration date. It is used to generate income while limiting risk.

VIX: The VIX Index, also known as the "Volatility Index" or "Fear Gauge," measures the market's expectation of future volatility based on the prices of S&P 500 index options. A higher VIX indicates that traders expect significant price swings in the near future, often associated with increased uncertainty or fear in the market.

Volatility Skew: Volatility skew refers to the pattern observed in the implied volatilities of options across different strike prices. It reflects the market's perception of future volatility and risk, often indicating higher implied volatility for out-of-the-money options compared to at-the-money options. Volatility skew is commonly used to assess market sentiment and potential price movements.

Volatility Surface: The volatility surface is a three-dimensional plot that represents the implied volatilities of options across different strike prices and expiration dates. It provides a comprehensive view of market expectations for future volatility, allowing traders and analysts to assess how volatility varies with respect to moneyness and time to expiration.

W

Wheel Strategy: The wheel strategy involves selling cash-secured puts until assigned, then selling covered calls on the acquired stock. It is an income-generating strategy that cycles between selling puts and calls.

Z

Z-Score: A Z-score measures the number of standard deviations a data point is from the mean of a data set. It is used to assess the likelihood of a data point occurring within a normal distribution.

TABLE OF FIGURES

Figure 1 - Long Call Payoff 15
Figure 2 - Short Call Payoff 16
Figure 3 - Long Put Payoff..18
Figure 4 - Short Put Payoff...20
Figure 5 - Call Option - Delta vs Underlying Price..26
Figure 6 - Put Option - Delta Vs Underlying Price..27
Figure 7 - Call/Put Option - Gamma vs Underlying Price.....................................31
Figure 8 - Call Option - Theta vs DTE 34
Figure 9 - Put Option - Theta vs DTE...34
Figure 10 - Call/Put Option - Vega vs Volatility 36
Figure 11 - Call Option - Rho vs Interest Rate...38
Figure 12 - Put Option - Rho vs Interest Rate 38
Figure 13 - SPY - Historical Volatility...42
Figure 14 - SPY - Implied Volatility..44
Figure 15 - Vertical Skew (IV vs Strike Price) - Simulated Data............................51
Figure 16 - Horizontal Skew (IV vs Days to Expiration) - Simulated Data 51
Figure 17 - Volatility Surface..54
Figure 18 - Covered Call Payoff..57
Figure 19 - Cash-Secured Put Payoff 58
Figure 20 - Covered Call Payoff..81
Figure 21 - Cash-Secured Put Payoff 97

BIBLIOGRAPHY

Bittman, R. (1998). *Trading index options*. McGraw-Hill.

Black, F., & Scholes, M. (1973). *The Pricing of Options and Corporate Liabilities*. Journal of Political Economy, 81(3), 637-654.

Carmona, R. (2014). *Statistical Analysis of Financial Data in R*. Springer.

Chen, D. A., Sebastian, M. (2011). *The Option Trader's Hedge Fund: A Business Framework for Trading Equity and Index Options*. Wiley.

Cohen, G. (2005). *The Bible of Options Strategies: The Definitive Guide for Practical Trading Strategies*. FT Press.

Cottle, C. M. (2006). *Option Trading: The Hidden Reality*. RiskDoctor.

Fama, E. F., & French, K. R. (2004). *The Capital Asset Pricing Model: Theory and Evidence*. Journal of Economic Perspectives.

Gibbs, R. M. (2014). *Profiting from Weekly Options: How to Earn Consistent Income Trading Weekly Option Serials*. FT Press.

Hull, J. C. (2018). *Options, Futures, and Other Derivatives (10th ed.)*. Pearson.

Jabbour, G., Budwick, P. (2004). *The option trader handbook: Strategies and trade adjustments*. Wiley Trading.

Jensen, M. C. (1968). *The Performance of Mutual Funds in the Period 1945-1964*. Journal of Finance.

Johnston, S.A. (2003). *Trading Options to Win: Profitable Strategies and Tactics for Any Trader*. Wiley.

Kaufman, P. J. (2013). *Trading Systems and Methods (5th ed.)*. Wiley.

Kraft, B. (2009). *The smart investor's money machine: Methods and strategies to create regular income*. Wiley Trading.

Lowell, L. (2007). *Get Rich with Options: Four Winning Strategies Straight from the Exchange Floor*. Wiley.

McMillan, L. G. (2012). *Options as a Strategic Investment (5th ed.)*. Prentice Hall Press.

Nations, S. (2010). *The Complete Book of Option Spreads and Combinations: Strategies for Income Generation, Directional Moves, and Risk Reduction*. McGraw-Hill Education.

Passarelli, D. (2011), *The Market Taker's Edge*. McGrawHill

Reilly, F. K., & Brown, K. C. (2012). *Investment Analysis and Portfolio Management (10th ed.)*. South-Western College Pub.

Rhoads, R. (2008). *Option spread trading: A comprehensive guide to strategies and tactics*. Wiley Trading.

Saliba, A., J. (2009). *Option Spread Strategies: Trading Up, Down, and Sideways Markets*. Bloomberg Press.

Sebastian, M. (2021). *Trading Options for Edge: Profit from Options and Manage Risk like the Professionals*. McGraw-Hill Education.

Sharpe, W. F. (1964). *Capital Asset Prices: A Theory of Market Equilibrium under Conditions of Risk*. Journal of Finance.

Smith, C. D. (2008). *Option Strategies: Profit-Making Techniques for Stock, Stock Index, and Commodity Options*. Wiley.

Taleb, N. N. (2010). *The Black Swan: The Impact of the Highly Improbable (2nd ed.)*. Random House.

Wolff, J. (2013). *The Stock Option Income Generator: How to Make Steady Profits by Renting Your Stocks*. Wiley Trading.

Wolinsky, M. C. (2010). *Put Option Strategies for Smarter Trading: How to Protect and Build Capital in Turbulent Markets*. FT Press

Yates, L. (2003). *High Performance Options Trading: Option Volatility & Pricing Strategies*. Wiley.

Zerenner, E., Chupka, M. (2008). *Naked Puts: Power Strategies for Consistent Profits*. Marketplace Books.

Data Sources

Yahoo Finance: *https://finance.yahoo.com/*

Nasdaq: *https://www.nasdaq.com/*

www.ingramcontent.com/pod-product-compliance
Lightning Source LLC
Chambersburg PA
CBHW052300220526
45471CB00001B/429